THE DAY
GOD LAUGHED

THE DAY GOD LAUGHED

Sayings, Fables and Entertainments
of the Jewish Sages

Chosen and translated by
HYAM MACCOBY

With conversations between
WOLF MANKOWITZ and HYAM MACCOBY

Illustrations by Cecily Ben-Tovim

ST. MARTIN'S PRESS
NEW YORK

For
Eva and Hilaire Geller

For information write:
St. Martin's Press Inc.,
175 Fifth Avenue, New York, N.Y. 10010

ISBN 0–312–18403–4

Library of Congress Catalog Card Number 78–53502
First published in the United States of America in 1978

Library of Congress Cataloging in Publication Data

Main entry under title:

The Day God laughed.

    1. Rabbinical literature—Translations into English.
2. Tales, Jewish. I. Maccoby, Hyam, 1924–
II. Mankowitz, Wolf.
BM495.D38   296.1′205′21   78–53502
ISBN 0–312–18403–4

Printed in Great Britain

CONTENTS

The Talmud must not be regarded as an ordinary book, composed of twelve volumes; it possesses absolutely no intrinsic similarity with any other literary production, but forms, without any figure of speech, a world of its own which must be judged by its own peculiar laws.

Heinrich Graetz,
History of the Jews, II, p. 639

Introduction

The English (Soncino) translation of the Talmud contains over 4,000,000 words—and this is only the Babylonian Talmud. There is, too, a shorter Palestinian Talmud. Also, there is a vast literature called the Midrash which is associated with the Talmud and can be called loosely part of the Talmudic literature.

The basic part of the Talmud is called the Mishnah, which in the English translation of H. Danby comprises about half a million words. The Mishnah was written down about 200 CE, but this was really an editing of earlier materials which had accumulated since about 150 BCE*. The rest of the Talmud, which is called Gemara, and consists of commentary on the Mishnah, was edited and completed about 500 CE. It consists of material that accumulated since the closing of the Mishnah.

Despite its great length, the main difficulty in studying the Talmud is its extreme brevity of expression. By the use of technical expressions, whole arguments are compressed into a few words. Really, the whole Talmud is in note form. The only other ancient literary works with which it can be compared, in this respect, are those of Aristotle, which are mostly in the form of compressed lecture-notes.

The major part of the Talmud consists of arguments between Rabbis, which took place over a period of 650 years. The arguments are mostly about points of Jewish religious law and ethics, and since this is all based ultimately on the Hebrew Bible (the Old Testament) many of these arguments turn on questions of interpretation of Biblical texts. In addition, how-

*BCE ('before the Common Era'), and CE ('Common Era') are used in this book instead of the Christian terms BC and AD.

ever, the Rabbis argued with each other on every subject under the sun: whether it would have been better for man not to have been born, whether the coming of the Messiah will be in the spring or the autumn, whether the Greek language is more beautiful than Hebrew, whether the Book of Job is fact or fiction, whether the world is round or square, whether the ratio between the diameter of a circle and its circumference is $3\frac{1}{3}$, and so on.

In the Talmud, the opinions of over one thousand Rabbis are quoted, belonging to seventeen successive generations. If an opinion is expressed on a matter of theology, poetry or science, the Talmud makes no attempt to lay down a final decision in the matter. But if the matter discussed is one of practical law or ethics, the Talmud endeavours to come to a conclusion, even if this can be reached only by taking a vote among a group of leading Rabbis. In such matters, it was held, it was better to be wrong than indecisive. It was never held that any decision of the Rabbis was infallible. Instead, it was held that God had given to the Rabbis the right of decision, whether right or wrong.

To become a Rabbi, one had to complete a rigorous course of training. Rabbis were not *priests*, but lay-leaders, well-versed in Jewish knowledge. Most Rabbis were poor men, and made their living by various trades and professions, e.g. wood-cutter, shoe-maker, carpenter, charcoal-burner, etc. Some Rabbis were rich. Some Rabbis were priests, for a priest (that is a descendant of the House of Aaron, privileged to serve in the Temple before it was destroyed by the Romans in 70 CE) could receive training as a Rabbi like any other man. Priesthood however, conferred no religious authority *per se:* 'A learned bastard takes precedence over an ignorant High Priest,' says the Mishnah.

One has to follow a Talmudic argument to its conclusion in order to see what the upshot is, i.e. what decision has been reached. Even then it is not always easy to discover what has been decided, and there is a voluminous literature dating from 500 CE to the present day on disputed points. Therefore, always beware when someone says, 'The Talmud says this' or 'The Talmud says that'. What he *should* say is that some *specific* Rabbi in the Talmud says this or that. Even if this

Rabbi has the decisive opinion, this is not necessarily final, because such decisions could be wrong, even though in accordance with 'the rule of law' they are regarded as being in force until they are proved wrong and officially repealed. The Talmud, in this sense, is an unfinished work, that is, an open-ended work which lays down a procedure but gives no final answers. As for matters of philosophical speculation or theological theorizing, the Talmud does not even attempt to provide final answers, but merely records varying opinions and arguments.

The Talmud was always regarded by the Jews as a holy and authoritative work, yet every sentence in it was regarded as subject to argument. This is rather like Bradley's definition of an Optimist as someone who says, 'This is the best of all possible worlds, and everything in it is a necessary evil.' Even the *refuted* arguments in the Talmud were regarded as holy, because what the Talmud consecrates is the process of argument itself.

Just as the Talmud regards the Bible as intelligent, so it regards all the Rabbis who take part in the Talmudic arguments as intelligent. Therefore, if a Rabbi is reported as saying something which is inconsistent with something he said on some other occasion (even if it is only the *implications* of a saying on one topic which appear to conflict with the implications of a saying by the same Rabbi on a different topic), the Talmud considers itself bound to clear up the apparent inconsistency, and will take endless trouble to show that the inconsistency is only apparent. Each Rabbi has his own characteristic viewpoint, which can be traced through many fields of law, ethics and theology, and though the viewpoints conflict at many points with each other, each must remain consistent with itself— otherwise the Rabbi would be no true Rabbi. So the many thousands of Rabbinical sayings in the Talmud are not just reports of isolated sayings. They are networks of related attitudes, each providing a consistent and comprehensive interpretation of the Talmudic system. The Talmudic student must study *all* these interlacing systems, so that he acquires not just one version of Judaism but a great many, covering a wide range of possibilities. But in fact, Judaism consists not of any one of these systems (though one may be adopted as the practical one to follow in any given era) but of the whole complex of systems. Studying the Talmud is like juggling with plates, each of which has to be kept spinning on the end of its upright rod—just as the juggler keeps going round his spinning plates in order to preserve their simultaneous motion, so the Talmud keeps going round its spinning systems, each belonging to a different Rabbi, in order to keep them all in good logical repair. This is why the Codes can never take the place of the Talmud (the Codes are the summaries of the Talmud, giving only the conclusions of the arguments, which were made chiefly in the Middle Ages).

How did the Talmud start? We can see some proto-Talmudic activity going on as early as the time of Ezra the Scribe (about 450 BCE), but the earliest fully Talmudic material dates from the origin of the movement known as Pharisaism. It was the Pharisaic movement that created the Talmud, in the period after 150 BCE. The Gospels have given the world a picture of the Pharisees which is almost wholly misleading. This unfavourable picture of the Pharisees as proud, hypocritical, upper-class oppressors of the poor is a travesty invented at a time later than that of Jesus, as part of the Church's campaign against the Jews. The actual Pharisees can be observed in the writings of Josephus and in the Talmud, and in the Jewish liturgy which was their creation. They formed one of the greatest spiritual and intellectual movements in history.

The leaders of the Pharisees were called Sages, or (later) Rabbis, and it is important to grasp that these leaders were not *priests*, but lay-leaders who came from every walk of life. The Priests were an entirely separate body of men, whose function was to perform the rites and ceremonies of the Temple. The Priests were an hereditary caste, being descended from Aaron the brother of Moses. One of the greatest achievements of the Pharisees was their demotion of the status of the Priests in Judaism. The Pharisees did not wish to abolish the Priests or the Temple, which remained the cultic centre of Jewish religion; but they brought about a separation between religious authority and the Temple cult. The Priests continued to perform the sacrifices, but they had no authority as religious teachers, even in Temple matters—for the Priests had to perform even the sacrifices in accordance with the instructions given to them by the Rabbis.

There was really nothing new about this in Judaism. The

prophets of the Old Testament were not priests, and often inveighed against the priesthood. The first and greatest of the prophets, Moses, was not a priest, and gave the office of High Priest to his brother Aaron, a comparative nonentity. But at certain periods, the priesthood did acquire great authority, and then it was necessary for a kind of revolt to be staged, or, more correctly, for the priesthood to be put back into its proper place. In the time of the Hellenistic domination of Judaea (after the death of Alexander the Great in 323 BCE), the High Priest acquired an unhealthy degree of spiritual and temporal power. A movement of those called the Hasidim opposed this power, and gave decisive support to the struggle for freedom from Hellenistic rule led by Judas Maccabaeus. The successors of the Hasidim were the Pharisees, who had to face further threats to Judaism from the Hasmonean king-priests who succeeded the early Maccabees. The Pharisees were thus the heirs to a long tradition of keeping priests (and kings) in their place. So far from being the Establishment figures represented in the New Testament caricature, the Pharisees were a permanent opposition party, who acted as watch-dogs on behalf of the Jewish people against any attempt to destroy the Mosaic Constitution, by which the power and authority of priests and kings were strictly limited. The Pharisees were also the guardians of national liberty, and were the leaders of the whole Resistance movement against the Romans, just as their predecessors, the Hasidim, had led the Resistance movement against the Greeks. (Jesus, by the way, was undoubtedly a Pharisee. Many of his sayings—for example, 'The Sabbath was made for man, not man for the Sabbath'—were well-known Pharisaic sayings. The alleged conflict between Jesus and the Pharisees is a politically-motivated myth.)

Opposed to the Pharisees was a small but powerful group called the Sadducees. This party consisted of a few High-Priestly families and rich land-owning families. Their religious allegiance was to three great institutions: the Temple, the Priesthood and the Written Law (Torah). They did not approve of the Pharisaic idea that the Written Law, though divinely-inspired, was only a basis for discussion, and that anyone at all, however basely-born, could join in this discussion on equal terms. Nor did the Sadducees approve of the Pharisaic idea that those who could discuss best were qualified to be the highest religious authorities in the land. The Sadducees thought that the Priests should be regarded as teachers and religious authorities, not merely as ceremonial officials—in fact, that the High Priest should have a role somewhat similar to that of the Pope in the Roman Catholic Church of later times.

In the times of the Hasmonean kings, the Sadducees were also great supporters of the monarchy (especially as in this period the institutions of the monarchy and the High Priesthood were combined). But when the Romans took over, and the monarchy was abolished, the Sadducees, always on the side of the Establishment, became supporters of the Roman occupying power—i.e. quislings. They accepted positions of authority under Roman rule, and became police officials and gauleiters, prepared to hand over to the Romans any troublemakers or Resistance-leaders who wished to restore Jewish independence. This was the situation at the time of Jesus. The High Priest at this time was the chief of the Sadducee party. He was appointed *by the Romans*, not by the Jews, and was in fact regarded by the Jews as a whole with contempt. It was this Sadducee quisling, Caiaphas, who handed over Jesus to the Romans as a trouble-maker. The Pharisees, even according to the biased Gospel accounts, had no part in the arrest of Jesus or his 'trial' (actually merely a police investigation) or his betrayal to the Romans.

Thus, in order to understand the Talmud, it is essential to understand its ideological background in the Pharisee movement (the name 'Pharisee', by the way, did not survive after 70 CE, when the Temple was destroyed, for the simple reason that the Sadducee party ceased to exist at that time, having no raison d'être without the Temple, so that the Pharisees became co-extensive with the Jewish people and did not any longer require a name to differentiate them from the Sadducees). The Talmud is the record of Pharisaic discussions because discussion was the very basis of Pharisaism. 'The Oral Law' (as opposed to the Written Law) was the name given by the Pharisees to the continuing tradition of discussion by which the Torah was related to the lives of men in each generation. The Talmud is the embodiment of the Oral Law as it manifested itself during seventeen Jewish generations.

14

Long before the time of Jesus, the Pharisees, in the course of their discussions, had introduced many reforms of the Jewish religion and law. For example, the well-known *lex talionis* ('an eye for an eye, a tooth for a tooth') had long been understood by them to mean that *compensation* had to be paid for any injury inflicted on a fellow human-being. Compensation had to be paid under four headings: injury, medical expenses, loss of employment, humiliation. The idea that physical retaliation could be regarded as a recognized legal process is ridiculed in the Pharisaic writings. What would happen, asks the Talmud, if a one-eyed man knocked out another man's eye?

It was the Pharisees, too, who were the founders of *congregationalism*. They invented the synagogue as a 'place of meeting', where each local community met in fellowship to pray and study the Law and listen to the sermon. In developing the technique of the sermon, the Pharisees invented the *parable*, with which Christians are familiar in the typically Pharisaic preaching of Jesus. The parable, with its vivid, homely content of seed-time, harvest, tenant and landlord, king's sons and journeys, conveyed the thought of the Pharisees to the common people; it was part of their campaign of *universal education*, which aimed at making every Jew learned in the Law and succeeded in stigmatizing illiteracy as a state unpleasing to God. The sermons of the Pharisees, based on the weekly portion of Law read in the synagogues on the Sabbath, are found in the Midrash and in the 'Aggadic' portions of the Talmud.

The word 'Law' (used in the previous sentence) is the usual translation (based on the New Testament Greek translation 'nomos') of the Hebrew word 'Torah', which was the name given to the Hebrew Bible, and particularly to the Five Books of Moses (the Pentateuch). But 'Law' is really a mistranslation, for 'Torah' does not mean 'Law' but 'Guidance' or 'Teaching'. The Bible contains a good deal of law, but it also contains many stories and much straight history. The Talmud, too, contains a great deal of law, but also many stories, parables, observations about ordinary life, and discussions about everything from astronomy to cooking. The legal part of the Talmud is called Halakhah (which might be translated as 'Going' or 'Way'), and the non-legal part is called Aggadah (which means literally 'Story-telling'). The Aggadah is not found segregated in any

15

particular part of the Talmud. It exists largely in the form of digressions, arising by a process of free-association out of the basic legal discussion which forms the skeleton of the Talmud. The loose form of the Talmud, consisting of a free-wheeling commentary on the Mishnah, allows for any number of digressions, so that Aggadah arises in very unexpected ways; for instance, an account of the rebellion of Bar Kochba arises out of legal discussion on the procedure of the Sanhedrin. In the Midrash, on the other hand, Aggadah forms the basis and Halakhah arises by digression. So in the Talmudic literature generally, Halakhah and Aggadah are two ever-present ingredients, mixed in varying proportions and in unpredictable fashion. The charm of the Talmud is partly the result of this unpredictability. When one turns a page, one is never sure what one is going to find: a knotty legal discussion, a story of the Rabbis, an explication of a Biblical passage, or perhaps a string of tall stories reminiscent of the Arabian Nights.

The legal side of the Talmud is subject to many misapprehensions. In Christianity, 'law' is a dirty word, being regarded as the antithesis of the spirit. The Law is thought of as a dead thing; as a fetter, inhibiting the free movement and decision of the spirit. All this is quite foreign to Pharisaic Judaism, in which the law is regarded as the supreme expression of love. To love one's neighbour, which, as Jesus pointed out, is the basic principle of Judaism, means that one should be much concerned with *justice*. The Law is the expression of the renunciation of private vengeance. It is the embodiment of the idea that even a criminal must be treated with love, for it is no longer the criminal who is being punished, but the crime. Loving one's enemies, or the enemies of society, was not a principle first thought of by Jesus, but is implied in every system of public justice, where each citizen is equal before the law, and no private hatreds are allowed scope. But the equation of justice and love is nowhere more explicit and conscious than in Judaism. The active pursuit of love of one's neighbour requires close consideration of all life-situations in which one's neighbour's welfare may be concerned. This is an enquiry which demands all one's faculties and intelligence. It is useless to rely on spontaneous good-will; for nothing is more common than to feel good-will without *knowing* how to put one's good-

16

will into effect. There is no conflict between knowing and doing; one's actions do not become unspontaneous and lifeless just because one is obeying the Law. It is not a question of obeying an unquestioned Law with sheep-like docility. It is a question of taking part in a continuous *process of legislation*, in which every member of society is expected to be involved. The whole Jewish people, in the Pharisaic view, had to acquire the Law and play on it like an instrument. Law was not something alien and oppressive; it was a communal cognitive enquiry, which was constantly developing and conquering new areas of life. The Christian idea that every act, in order to be morally valid, has to be a new creation, a spontaneous reaction of grace, condemns morality to a perpetual state of barbarous simplicity. No communally-directed development is possible. It is as if every mathematician were required to discover all the theorems of Euclid for himself, so that mathematics has to start afresh in every generation. The Christian condemnation of the Law, as found in the Epistles of Paul, meant that the moral discoveries of the Pharisees were lost to Christendom, so that, for example, fifteen hundred years after Jesus, Christian judges were still unaware of the immorality of extorting evidence by torture. The abolition of Law does not result in angelic behaviour arising from the spontaneous Law of Grace. Law cannot be abolished, because it is a necessary part of being human. If you abolish Law, what you get is not Grace, but bad Law. If you expel Law from religion, what you get is irreligious Law.

The Talmud is singularly devoid of Great Men, in the sense of outstanding isolated Heroes. The Rabbis were not Heroes or demi-gods. In this respect, the Talmud is very different from the Gospels, where there is really only one Figure, and everyone else is dwarfed into insignificance. In the Talmud there are swarming crowds of figures, all engaged in a communal endeavour. The Rabbis called each other by the honourable name 'Haver' which means 'Comrade'; it is the aim of the Talmud that 'all Israel should become comrades' (*haverim kol Yisrael*), not that they should submerge their identity into some towering god-figure. The Law is the protector of individuality, idiosyncrasy, the quirks of the differentiated personality. This is the origin of the quaintness of the Talmud. It lacks the kind of elevated nobility which is characteristic of hierarchical literature. The Talmud is never on a high horse. Every Rabbi is nothing more, and nothing less, than a man.

Excellent anthologies of the Talmud already exist, but they all strike a rather solemn, elevated note which is misleading. The Talmud certainly has its solemn, elevated moments, but its atmosphere, in general, is more relaxed. It is the atmosphere of the synagogue, rather than of the Temple. The synagogue is a place for discussion, even for gossip, not for the high drama of ritual and sacrifice. In the synagogue, voices may be raised in heated debate, jokes or stories may be told, displays of individual temperament may take placed, even though the main tone of communication is earnest and purposeful.

But the fact that this relaxed synagogal atmosphere exists in Judaism is itself significant; it is a point of theological importance, arising from the essence of Judaism itself. Judaism does not stand over against the world. Nothing in the world is alien to it. Somewhere in the Talmud will be found references to every common object or being in the world—not only ships and kings and sealing-wax, but alleys and anaesthetics and bracelets and briars and coals and cows and dates and deaf-mutes and eggs and eye-balls and fairs and fevers. . . . One could go through the alphabet for ever. There is a story about a Yeshivah student who was persuaded one day to take a rest from his Talmud studies and visit the countryside. As he walked through a farmyard, he saw a strange little animal, and asked, 'What is that?' He was told that it was a hen. 'Ah!' he cried in mystic delight. 'It is the holy *tarnegoles* from the Talmud!' (Actually, he said 'from the Gemorra'—one of the awkward things about the Talmud is that its most devoted students never call it the 'Talmud'.)

To be so impressed by the holiness of ordinary things that one forgets to go and look at them is perhaps going too far. It is like an Irishman I once knew who only knew about daffodils through the work of James Joyce. But ordinary things do suffer a sea-change in the 'Sea of the Talmud'. They become subject to quaint or solemn or tortuous discussions, until they find themselves taking part in the dance of the Law, like the animals in *Alice in Wonderland*. And it is not only that the objects of the world are brought into the dance; but the dance itself is continually conducted in terms of the objects of the

18

world. Thus important distinctions in the law of Torts are given such names as Horn and Foot and Tooth; and the measurements required for certain legal purposes are, more often than not, 'as much as an egg', or 'as much as an olive', or 'as much as can be sown with a basketful of barley-seed'. There is a kind of interchange between the abstract and the concrete of the kind that Ezra Pound thought that he had found in the Chinese ideograms (though unfortunately he took the Talmud, without ever having looked into it, as the type of the abstract divorced from the concrete).

This collection seeks to convey something of the special flavour of the Talmud: its combination of the earthy and the spiritual, the concrete and the abstract. There is here, of course, a difference of philosophy between Judaism and other religions. Judaism is a religion of the body. Even immortality is conceived in terms of the resurrection of the body, not in terms of a so-clean wraith-like soul floating clear from the contamination of matter. Judaism never thinks of the body as getting in the way of the spiritual life. On the contrary, the body is the instrument and subject-matter of the spiritual life; as well say that stars get in the way of the study of astronomy. The meaning of *law* is the civilization of the body; those who wish to have religion without law really wish to have religion without body. The feeling of wonder in Judaism is for the body; a morning prayer expresses this: 'Blessed art thou O Lord our God, King of the Universe, who hast formed man in wisdom and created him as a complex of hollow tubes' (literally: 'tubes, tubes, hollow, hollow'). It is the body that performs actions, and actions are the subject-matter of religion. The body is a divine tour de force, an incomplete work of art which it is our business on earth to complete, so sharing in the work of God the Artist.

This being so, there are bound to be many things in the Talmud (as in the Old Testament) which seem to people brought up in the 'spiritual' religions to be crude or 'materialistic' or laughably quaint. It has seemed natural for Jewish anthologists, aware of such reactions, to play down this aspect of the Talmud—to censor out, for example, the prostitute's fart in the story included here. The present collection is an attempt to avoid this attitude of shame, and to present the Talmud as

19

it really is, perhaps even at the risk of going too much to the opposite extreme. At any rate, we hope that something of the *gusto* of the Talmud will be conveyed—the gusto which derives from the whole-hearted acceptance of life on this earth as God-given, and expresses itself in a Rabelaisian exploration of the possibilities of the body, including the pleasure of exploration itself, with its heady excitements of argument, disagreement, contest, and intellectual mastication.

One other aspect of the Talmud must be mentioned in this Introduction. It is an aspect which contributes an element of pathos and poetry. One of the main motivations of the Talmud is a kind of *nostalgia*. The Talmud arose when the Jewish State was lost; the whole Talmud can be seen as a prolonged effort to remember what it was like to be a functioning community with political independence, giving a full implementation to Judaism as a political and social organism. Everything had to be recorded and remembered: how the first-fruits were brought up to Jerusalem; how the Sanhedrin was constituted, and what was its procedure; how the service of the Temple was carried on; the exact dimensions of the Temple and its architectural plan; the rights and duties of a Jewish king; all the things which could not be put into practice in the circumstances of Exile had to be kept in good mental repair so that when Elijah and the Messiah arrived to lead back the Jews to their ancestral land, they would know exactly how things ought to be done. From this aspect, the Talmud should be thought of as analogous to such a work as Plato's *Republic*, or Sir Thomas More's *Utopia*—a blue-print for the future, when humankind would come into its own. For the coming of the Messiah would be an event significant not for the Jews alone but for the whole human race. And here, perhaps, is the deepest lesson of the Talmud and of Judaism: that there is no conflict between the particular and the universal, for, on the contrary, they imply each other. The full realization of the particular is the triumph of the universal. The central paradox which the Talmud reconciles is that while God is infinite and unimaginable, man was made in the image of God.

H M

20

ENJOYING LIFE

Enjoying Nature

BLESSINGS

On seeing trees blossoming for the first time in the year:

Blessed art Thou, Lord our God, King of the universe, who has made His world lacking in nothing, and has created good creatures and good trees to delight with them the children of men.

Berakhot, 43b

On seeing the sea:

Blessed art Thou, Lord our God, King of the universe, who made the great sea.

On seeing beautiful or striking flowers or trees or animals:

Blessed art Thou, Lord our God, King of the universe, who has such as these in His world.

Against Asceticism

SOME SAYINGS

Said Rabbi Eliezer ha-Kappar: 'A Nazarite is called a sinner because he deprived himself of wine.'

Said Samuel: 'Whoever engages continually in fasting is called a sinner.'

Ta'anit, 11a

Said Rav: 'On Judgment Day, a man will have to give account for every good thing which his eye saw and he did not enjoy.'

Palestinian Talmud, Kiddushin, end

The world is a wedding

Said Samuel to Rav Judah: 'Shinena [Rav Judah's nickname, probably means "Toothy"], hurry up and eat, hurry up and drink, for the world from which we must go is like a wedding-feast.'

Eruvin, 54a

24

Physical Beauty & Strength

Rabbi Johanan said, 'I alone remain of the beautiful men of Jerusalem.'

He who desires to see the beauty of Rabbi Johanan should take a silver goblet while it is still glowing with the heat of the crucible, fill it with the seeds of red pomegranate, encircle its brim with a garland of red roses, and set it between the sun and the shade. That glow gives some impression of the beauty of Rabbi Johanan.

Rabbi Johanan used to go and sit at the gates of the ritual bath. 'When the daughters of Israel ascend from the bath, purified for intercourse with their husbands,' he said, 'let them look upon me, that they may bear sons as beautiful as I, and as learned in the Torah as I.'

Bava Metsia, 84a

Note. Rabbi Johanan's praise of his own beauty is not vanity, but a celebration of God's creation, an elegy on the departed glories of Jerusalem, and a trust to be used for the benefit of humanity.

WHY THEY WEPT

Rabbi Eleazar fell ill, and Rabbi Johanan went to visit him. Rabbi Eleazar was lying in a dark room, but Rabbi Johanan bared his arm, and such was the beauty of Rabbi Johanan that the room became full of light.

Rabbi Johanan then noticed that Rabbi Eleazar was weeping.

25

'Why do you weep?' he asked. 'Is it because you feel that you have not acquired enough knowledge of the Torah in your span of life? Have we not learnt, "Whether a man achieves much or little, it is all one, as long as he directs his heart to God"?'

Said Rabbi Eleazar, 'No; I am weeping because of your beauty, which must one day rot in the earth.'

'Ah,' said Rabbi Johanan, 'for that you are quite right to weep.'

So they sat and wept together.

Berakhot, 5b

TWO FAT MEN

Rabbi Ishmael ben Yosi and Rabbi Eleazar ben Simeon were both very fat men. Their bellies were so round that when they met each other and stood talking together, a herd of oxen could have gone between them, under their bellies, and not touched either of them.

Once a Roman lady taunted them, saying, 'Your children must have been begotten by some other men. How can men with bellies such as yours beget children?'

They answered her, 'Our wives' bellies are even huger than ours.'

Said she, 'That makes it all the more likely that your children were begotten by some other men.'

There is some difference of opinion as to what they then replied. Some say they quoted the verse, 'According to the man is his power' [Judges, 8: 21]. Others say they replied, 'Love overcomes the flesh.'

But why did they reply to her at all? Does not Scripture say, 'Do not answer a fool in his folly'? [Proverbs, 26: 4]. They replied to her to prevent their children from being regarded as bastards.

Said Rabbi Johanan, 'Rabbi Ishmael's penis was like a wine-skin of nine Kavs' capacity.'

Rav Pappa said, 'Rabbi Johanan's penis was like a wine-skin

26

of five Kav's capacity.' Some report him as giving the measure-
ment as three Kavs' capacity.

And what about Rav Pappa himself? His penis was like a
Harpanian jug.

Bava Metsia, 84a

*Note. This Rabelaisian passage has caused great embarrassment
to some Talmud commentators. Goldschmidt, the translator of
the Talmud into German, laboured to prove that the word 'penis'
(literally 'member') can sometimes mean 'waist'. This chaste
suggestion is adopted in the Soncino Talmud (the translation
into English, edited by Isadore Epstein). The trouble is that
while a penis of nine Kavs is a very large penis, a waist of nine
Kavs is not large at all. (A Kav is equal to about 1¼ pints.) This
would make Rabbi Ishmael's penis equal to 11¼ pints capacity,
but this, as the analogy of a wine-skin would suggest, would be
at full erection.*

*Another desperate suggestion (by Jastrow) is that the word
eyvra (penis) could mean 'meal', and the passage is thus concerned with the Rabbis' appetite for food. Philologically, both
these suggestions are unconvincing. Moreover, there is the obvious
intention in the passage to enlarge on the text, 'According to
the man is his power,' and to show that the Rabbis, despite their
huge bellies, were able to engage in intercourse because of the
proportionate hugeness of their penises.*

*Medieval commentators did not doubt that the word eyvra
meant 'penis' as usual, and explained that 'the greater the man,
the greater is his sexual appetite', a sentiment more congenial
to moralists of the twentieth century than to those of the nine-
teenth.*

*For further comment on the passage, see the conversation
between Mankowitz and Maccoby on page 91.*

THE DAUGHTERS OF ISRAEL

It once happened that a man vowed not to marry his niece, and
later repented of his vow.

Rabbi Ishmael (who made a practice of providing cosmetics

and adornments for the daughters of the poor), had the girl brought into his house, and beautified her.

He summoned the man and showed him the girl. Said Rabbi Ishmael, 'If you had known that she could have been as beautiful as this, would you have made the vow?'

Said the man, 'No.'

So Rabbi Ishmael released him from his vow.

In that same hour, Rabbi Ishmael wept, saying, 'The daughters of Israel are beautiful, but poverty destroys their beauty.'

When Rabbi Ishmael died, the daughters of Israel sang a lament, 'Daughters of Israel, weep over Rabbi Ishmael!'

So too it is said of King Saul, 'Daughters of Israel, weep over Saul, who clothed you in scarlet and ornaments of gold.'

Mishnah, Nedarim, 9: 10

Eating and Drinking

BEER OR WINE?

The question was raised, 'Must one make Kiddush [Sanctification of Sabbath] with wine, or may one use beer?'

Levi once sent some beer to Rabbi. The beer was very concentrated and Rabbi found the flavour excellent. He said, 'This beer is suitable for Kiddush, and moreover it is fitting to say over it all the songs and praises in the world.'
That night, however, Rabbi was in pain. 'This beer is treacherous,' he said.

Rabbi Joseph said, 'I will take a solemn vow not to drink beer.'

Pesachim, 107

THE FRUIT OF GENESSARETH

Rabbah bar bar Hanah said: 'When we went after Rabbi Johanan to eat the fruit of Genessareth, we used to bring him basket after basket of the fruit. When there were a hundred disciples present, we used to bring him ten each; and when there were only ten disciples present, we used to bring him a hundred each; and a basket of three se'ahs could hardly hold a hundred. Yet he would eat them all, and say, 'I swear I have not tasted anything.'
Rabbi Abbahu used to eat the fruit of Genessareth until his

29

skin grew so smooth that a fly could not retain a foothold on his forehead.

Rabbi Simeon Ben Lakish once ate so much of them that his mind began to wander, and Rabbi Johanan told the household of the Nasi, and Rabbi Judah the Prince sent out a search-party for him and brought him home.

Berakhot, 44a

Rab said: 'A meal without salt is no meal.' Rabbi Hiyya bar Abba said in the name of Rabbi Johanan: 'A meal without gravy is no meal.'

Rejoicing

THE JUGGLERS

He who has never seen the Rejoicing of the House of Water-drawing (on the feast of Tabernacles in the Temple) has never seen rejoicing in his life.

They said about Rabban Simeon ben Gamaliel that when he took part in the Rejoicing of the House of Water-drawing, he used to take eight fiery torches and juggle with them in the air, and not one of them would touch another.

There was not a courtyard in Jerusalem that did not reflect the light of the House of Water-drawing. The Hasidim and Men of Deed used to dance before them with fiery torches in their hands, singing songs and praises.

He who has never seen Jerusalem in her glory has never seen a beautiful city in his life. He who has not seen the Temple when it was standing, has never seen a remarkable building.

Succah, 53a

THE SEVENTH BLESSING

Blessed art thou our God, King of the Universe, who created joy and gladness, bridegroom and bride, mirth, song, delight and cheer, love and harmony, and peace and companionship. Soon, Lord our God, may be heard in the cities of Judah and in the streets of Jerusalem, the voice of joy and the voice of gladness, the voice of the bridegroom and the voice of the bride, the jubilant voices of the espoused from their wedding-

31

canopy and the young people from their feast of singing. Blessed art thou our Lord, who rejoices the bridegroom with the bride.

Ketuvot, 8a

Note. This is the concluding Blessing of the Seven Blessings sung over a goblet of wine at a wedding. The blessings are first found in the Talmud.

Studying

Beruriah once came across a student who was studying in a quiet, listless manner.

She gave him a kick, and said, 'When you study, you should study with all the 248 limbs of your body.'

Eruvin, 53b

Note. For Beruriah, the woman rabbi, see page 105*f.*

BEGINNING A LECTURE

Rabbah, before he began his lecture to his disciples, used to make jokes, so that his disciples would feel cheerful.

After a while, he would sit in silent awe, and then begin his lecture.

Pesachim, 117a

A CONVERSATION ON ASCETICISM

MANKOWITZ   Some of these sayings contain whole philosophies. I've always loved this one: 'Rav said, "On Judgment Day, a man will have to give account for every good thing which his eye saw and he did not enjoy." ' I think that's a magnificent philosophy.

MACCOBY   Yet asceticism does have some place in Judaism.

33

There's a kind of dialectic here. On the one hand, there are certain aspects of Judaism which are ascetic; yet at the same time, this asceticism is somehow turned into a kind of celebration. For example, the dietary laws are certainly ascetic; by depriving themselves of certain kinds of food, the Jews show themselves to be a kind of dedicated people, like an order of priests or an order of monks, who fast or avoid meat on certain days. But because you are only allowed certain kinds of food, therefore the kinds of food that you are allowed have to be cooked better than anybody ever cooked them before. And so, in the end, you get Jewish cooking, which arises out of an original asceticism.

MANKOWITZ   So asceticism really goes into the discussion under the culinary section.

MACCOBY   Yes, and that is true in another way, too. A true ascetic values and appreciates what he is giving up—otherwise he is not really sacrificing anything. The Talmud does not say that pork is forbidden because it's dirty or unhealthy. The Talmud says that pork is the finest food there is. Why, then, aren't we allowed to eat it? Because it's an ascetic regulation—one of those rules which people give themselves when they feel themselves to be a dedicated people—just as the Pythagoreans wouldn't eat beans.

MANKOWITZ   How did the rabbis who said this know it was a fact?

MACCOBY   There could be several answers to that. The Midrash says that a certain fish called the *shibuta*, which means either mullet or sturgeon, tastes like pork, and acts as a compensation to the Jews for not being allowed to eat pork.

MANKOWITZ   But how did the rabbis know that the *shibuta* tastes like pork, if they had never actually tasted pork?

MACCOBY   They could learn this fact from non-Jews who, in Jewish law, are allowed to eat pork, since the

34

dietary laws were given only to the Jews. Or you could even say that the Jews learnt this from their non-Jewish ancestors, such as Noah, or even from Abraham, who was allowed to eat pork, since he lived before the law was given. Or some rabbi might have learnt this from personal acquaintance, if he happened to fall ill and the doctor prescribed pork as a medicine, in which case it was permissible to eat it.

MANKOWITZ   I thought you might say that.

MACCOBY   Best of all, you could say that the rabbis felt on *a priori* principles that the dietary laws were not merely hygienic, but involved self-sacrifice and asceticism.

MANKOWITZ   The grass is always greener if you can't have it, and therefore pork must be the most delicious food in the world, just because you're not allowed to eat it.

MACCOBY   Yes, there could be something of that attitude. It's a better attitude, at any rate, than a sour-grapes attitude which might have said, 'We don't eat pork because it is disgusting rubbish—good enough for Gentiles, but not good enough for Jews.' On the contrary, there is even a minority opinion in the Talmud that the forbidden foods, including pork, will become permissible to Jews in the World to Come, as a reward for their self-denial in This World. This implies that pork is forbidden because it is too good for this imperfect world, and must be reserved for a better world, when all kinds of culinary delights will be served up, including the great fish Leviathan.

MANKOWITZ   I always have a theory—there's no justification for it at all apart from a kind of ethnographic hint here and there—about this non-eating of pork, which really derives, in my theory, from the fact that wherever human flesh is eaten throughout Polynesia and elsewhere, it is always described as 'long pig'. Man was frequently a cannibal in history and pre-history. In the area of Asia Minor there must have been enormous meat shortages before agriculture, and there must have been enormous incidence of cannibalism. And I think that one of the reasons why pig is forbidden is because it is so like human flesh.

MACCOBY   And because it is a smooth animal which has a kind of skin which is similar to that of a human being.

MANKOWITZ   My father knew in Africa one of the last of the Basuto chiefs who had eaten human flesh. And he talked with him extensively about this. The old man had become a Christian and he was forever condemning cannibalism, saying with self-reproach, 'When I was a boy, I ate men and fingers.' One day, whilst he was saying this, my father said to him, 'What did it taste like?', and he said, 'It was delicious.'

MACCOBY   I think that many of the prohibitions in Judaism were made not because the things prohibited were regarded as evil or unhealthy, but because they were regarded as too holy for ordinary use. The prohibition against pig may have been an instance of this, originally. We know that the Egyptian priests had a prohibition against eating pig, but once a year they had a great sacred pig-feast. Later, the pig-feast was discontinued, but the prohibition against eating pig continued, and the pig began to be regarded as an unclean animal. A similar development probably occurred in Judaism. Another example is *shaatnez*—the prohibition in the Bible against wearing a garment containing a mixture of wool and linen—all orthodox Jews even today observe this law, and go to a Jewish tailor to make sure that their clothes are made without any mixture of wool and linen. If you study the matter, you find that the curtains of the Temple were made of this mixture, and so were the vestments of the High Priest. Even the *tsitsis*, which is the priestly garment of the ordinary Jew, had this mixture in it in olden times. So the reason why the mixture is forbidden is because it is considered too holy a mixture for ordinary use.

STORIES

Folk Tales

THE EMPEROR HADRIAN AND THE OLD MAN

The Emperor Hadrian (may his bones be ground to dust) was walking in the paths near Tiberias, and he saw an old man digging holes to plant trees.

Said Hadrian, 'Old man, old man, if you had worked in the morning, you would not have to work in the evening.'

Said the old man, 'I worked in the morning, and now I work in the evening, and the Lord of the Heavens does what pleases him.'

Said Hadrian, 'By your life, old man, how old are you this day?'

Said he, 'I am a hundred years old.'

Said Hadrian, 'You are a hundred years old and you stand there digging holes to plant trees! Do you expect to eat their fruit?'

Said he, 'I shall eat the fruit if my merits are sufficient. If not, I toil for my descendants, as my fathers toiled for me.'

Said Hadrian, 'By your life, if you are privileged to eat their fruit, come and let me know.'

After some time, the trees produced figs. Said the old man, 'Now is the time to let the Emperor know.'

What did he do? He filled a basket with figs and went and stood by the gate of the palace.

They said to him, 'What is your business?'

He said to them, 'To go before the Emperor.'

When they brought him in, the Emperor said to him, 'What is your business?'

Said the old man, 'I am the old man whom you met when I was digging holes to plant trees. You said to me that if I was privileged to eat of them I should let you know. I have lived to eat of them, and these figs are of their fruit.'

Said the Emperor Hadrian in that hour: 'This is our command. Set up a chair of gold, and let him sit in it.'

Said the Emperor: 'This is our command. Empty this basket of his, and fill it with gold pieces.'

His servants said to him, 'Do you give so much honour to this old Jew?'

Said he, 'His Creator has honoured him. Shall I not honour him?'

The wife of the old man's neighbour was malicious and cunning. She said to her husband, 'Good-for-nothing! Can't you see that this Emperor likes figs and gives gold pieces for them?'

What did he do? He filled a bag with figs, and went and stood before the palace.

They said to him, 'What is your business?'

He said to them, 'I have heard that the Emperor loves figs and exchanges them for gold pieces.'

They went in and told the Emperor, 'An old man is standing at the gate of the palace carrying a bag full of figs. We said to him, "What is your business?" and he said to us, "I have heard that the Emperor loves figs and exchanges them for gold pieces." '

Said the Emperor: 'This is my command: place him in front of the gate of the palace, and everyone who goes in or goes out shall throw the figs in his face.'

Towards evening, they let him go and he went home. He said to his wife, 'According to all this honour which I received I will repay you.'

Said she, 'Go and boast to your mother that they were figs and not lemons, that they were ripe and not hard.'

Midrash, Leviticus Rabbah, 25, 5

Note. The name of the Emperor Hadrian is followed by the routine imprecation 'May his bones be ground to dust', even though the story shows him in a favourable light. Hadrian was the Emperor who put down the revolt of Bar Kochba with great slaughter, and afterwards tried to obliterate Judaism. He built a temple to Jupiter on the site of the Jewish Temple and renamed Jerusalem Aelia Capitolina. Previously, however, he had shown friendliness to Jewish sages, and is often represented in the Talmud in conversation with Rabbi Joshua ben Hanania.

THE JEWISH SHERLOCK HOLMES

Once an Athenian came to Jerusalem to study wisdom. He tried for three and a half years, without much success.

After the three and a half years, he bought a Jewish slave. He discovered, however, that the slave was blind in one eye.

He cried in disgust, 'I have studied for three and a half years to acquire wisdom, yet when I buy a slave, he turns out to be blind in one eye!'

Said the seller, 'By your life, the slave can see further with one eye than some people with two.'

The Athenian set out on the journey back to his home, together with his slave. When they came out of the gate, the slave said, 'Hurry, that we may overtake the caravan in front of us.'

The Athenian could not see any caravan, and asked, 'Where is the caravan?'

'It is four miles in front of us,' said the slave. 'There is a she-camel in it, which is blind in one eye. She has twins in her womb, and she is carrying two skin-bottles, one containing wine and the other vinegar. The camel-driver is a Gentile.'

Said the Athenian, 'O stiff-necked people! How can you tell with your one eye that the she-camel has one eye?'

Said the slave, 'I see that one side of the path has been grazed, but not the other side.'

'And how do you know that she has twins in her womb?'

'I can see the double depression in the earth where she lay down.'

'And how do you know that she is carrying two skin-bottles, one containing wine and one containing vinegar?'

'From the drippings. Wine soaks into the ground, and vinegar leaves bubbles.'

'And how do you know that the camel-driver is a Gentile?'

'Because he urinated in the middle of the road, and a Jew would urinate at the side of the road.'

'And how do you know that the caravan is four miles in front of us?'

43

'The camel's hooves are just perceptible. A camel's hoof-marks become imperceptible after four miles.'

Midrash, Lamentations Rabbah, I. 1, 12

Note. This story shows the cultural rivalry between the Jews and the Athenians, the two main claimants to 'wisdom' in the Greco-Roman Empire. Many such jocular tales of the discomfiture of the clever Athenians are found in the Talmudic writings. In this story, the Athenian finds that even a one-eyed Jewish slave can see further than he can.

Tall Stories

OG THE GIANT

How tall was Moses? Ten cubits. When he fought against the giant Og, king of Bashan, he took an axe ten cubits long. He rushed at Og, and jumped ten cubits in the air, and wounded Og fatally in the ankle.

When a man sees the stone with which Og, king of Bashan sought to destroy Israel, he should give thanks and praise to God. How do we know about this stone? It is a tradition. Og enquired, 'How big is the camp of Israel?' He was told, 'Three parasangs.' So he said, 'I will go and uproot a mountain three parasangs long and throw it on them, and kill them.' He went and uprooted a mountain three parasangs long and lifted it over his head to throw it. But the Holy One, Blessed be He, sent worms which bored holes in the mountain and it fell round his neck. He started to lift it off, but his teeth grew to this side and to that side, so that he could not draw it away; and that is what is meant by the verse in the Psalms [3: 8] 'You have broken the teeth of the wicked.'

Berakhot, 54b

Note. This last story was quoted by the apostate Nicholas Donin, at the Disputation at Paris, 1240, which led to the burning of the Talmud. Donin quoted the passage to prove the absurdity of the Talmud, but Rabbi Yehiel replied that this was merely one of the 'characteristic exaggerations' of the Talmud, which were not intended to be taken seriously.

THE JEWISH SINBAD

Rabbah bar bar Hanah is the Sinbad the Sailor of the Talmud.

45

His traveller's tales can only be described as whoppers, but some of them can be seen as parables or allegories; all of them show a Gargantuan quality of imagination and sense of wonder. Yet it is typical of the Talmudic world that Rabbah bar bar Hanah was also a master of the sober work of radical, Halakhic* thinking. As a pupil of the great Rabbi Johanan, he handed on many of his master's teachings, and contributed to the development of Halakhic discussion.

Said Rabbah bar bar Hanah, 'I myself saw with my own eyes a frog as big as Fort Hagronia. (How big is Fort Hagronia? Sixty houses.) There came along a snake and swallowed the frog. Then came a raven and swallowed the snake. Then the raven flew away and sat on the branch of a tree. Imagine how strong that branch must have been!'

Said Rav Pappa bar Samuel: 'If I hadn't been there, I wouldn't have believed it.'

And Rabbah bar bar Hanah said, 'It once happened that we were sailing in a ship and we saw a fish which had died because a mud-eater had settled in its nostrils. The fish was carried by the waves to the shore, and so huge was it that sixty cities were laid in ruins by the impact. Sixty cities fed from its flesh and sixty cities salted its flesh for future eating, and from the globe of one of its eyes they filled three hundred kegs of oil. When we returned after twelve months, we saw that they were fashioning from the bones shelters and dwelling-places to rebuild the sixty cities.'

And Rabbah bar bar Hanah said, 'Once we were sailing in a ship and we saw a fish that had sandy soil on its back with reeds growing out of it. We thought it was an island, so we landed on it and baked and cooked our food on it. When it felt its back getting too hot, it turned over, and if the ship had not been near, we would all have drowned.'

Said Rabbah bar bar Hanah, 'Once we were voyaging in a ship. We saw a bird standing up to its ankles in the water, with its head reaching the sky. We thought that the water must be shallow, so we decided to bathe in it to cool ourselves.

At this, a heavenly voice called out, "Do not bathe in the

*See Introduction, p. 15f.

water. Seven years ago an axe was dropped into that water, and it has not reached the bottom yet." '

Said Rav Ashi, 'That bird is the one that is called in the Psalms "Ziz-Sadai"* [Psalms, 50: 11].'

Bava Batra, 73b

THE CORPSES IN THE DESERT

Said Rabbah bar bar Hanah, 'Once we were travelling in the desert. A certain Arab merchant joined us. He was a remarkable man. By picking up some sand and smelling it, he could tell us our exact location—how far to one place, and in which direction, and how far to another place.

We said to him, "How far are we from water?"

He said, "Give me some sand."

We gave him some, and he smelt it. Then he said, "Eight parasangs."

Later we gave him some more sand, and he told us that we were now three parasangs from water.

To test him, I gave him some sand that I had secretly gathered further back. He smelt it and said, "This sand was not gathered here." Finally, we came to water just where he said it would be.

He said to me, "Come with me, and I will show you the corpses of the Israelites who died in the Wilderness."

We travelled together for a while, till we came to a certain region of the desert where we saw the corpses of the Israelites who died in the Wilderness. They were so well-preserved that they looked as if they had been embalmed. They lay on their backs, and one of them had his knee raised. The Arab merchant passed under this knee, riding on his camel, holding his spear upright, and did not touch the knee; this shows how huge these corpses were. The corpses were wearing the fringes with the purple thread, as prescribed by the Law [Numbers, 15: 38].

*The expression 'Ziz-Sadai' occurs only once in the Bible and its meaning is uncertain. The New English Bible translates (tentatively)'the teeming life of the fields'. Since the first part of the verse refers to birds ('I know all the fowls of the mountains'), Rav Ashi suggests that 'Ziz-Sadai' is the name of a bird, probably an extraordinary one such as that described in the story.

I cut off one fringe, and then found that we were unable to move away from the area.

Said the Arab merchant, "If you have taken anything from them, return it, for he who takes anything from them cannot move away." So I returned it, and then we were able to move away.

Later when I told this story to the Rabbis, they said, "What a fool and an ass is Rabbah bar bar Hanah! Why did you cut off the fringe? You should have examined it where it was, and then you would have been able to decide the dispute between the House of Shammai and the House of Hillel about the correct number of threads and joints in the ritual fringes."

Then the Arab merchant said to me, "Come with me, and I will show you Mount Sinai." We travelled until we came to Mount Sinai, and I saw that it was surrounded by scorpions as huge as white asses. Then I heard a heavenly voice saying, "Woe is me, for I have made an oath, and who will release me from my oath?"

Later, when I told this story to the Rabbis, they said, "What a fool and an ass is Rabbah bar bar Hanah! This was the voice of God, seeking release from his oath to send Israel into exile. If you had only pronounced the prescribed formula, *Mufar lakh* ['Thy oath is void'], God would have been released from His oath, and the exile would have come to an end." '

(And why indeed did Rabbah bar bar Hanah omit to say *Mufar lakh*? Because he thought that the oath which God was regretting was perhaps His oath not to bring another Flood upon the earth [Genesis, 9: 11 and Isaiah, 54: 9]. And how were the Rabbis so sure that the oath concerned the exile and not the Flood? Because if it concerned the Flood, why should He say, 'Woe is me'?)

Bava Batra, 73b

Note. This last story of Rabbah bar bar Hanah was cited in a medieval Disputation at Paris (1240) as an example of the blasphemies of the Talmud. After the Disputation, twenty-five cart-loads of copies of the Talmud were burnt by the Christian authorities who had organized the Disputation; yet the Talmud continued to be taught in Paris, since some Rabbis knew it by heart. That God should say, 'Woe is me,' and that He should be absolved of His oath by a human being, seemed to the Christians a great derogation of His dignity. God is often portrayed in the Talmud as suffering for the exile of His people; and the idea of a suffering God should not be shocking to Christians, of all people (though, in fact, Christian theology held that God the Father was 'impassible', and only God the Son could suffer). That God could be absolved of an oath by a human being is a daring conception, but only continues the thought of the Old Testament, in which God is upbraided by Abraham for being unjust (Genesis, 18: 25), and is persuaded by Moses to change His mind (Exodus, 32: 14). This kind of human influence on God at least refutes the opposite kind of charge often made against Biblical and Talmudic Judaism, that they regard God as transcendently remote.

THE PRINCE OF THE DEMONS

Solomon had to build the Temple without iron tools. He said to the Rabbis, 'How shall I manage?'

They replied, 'You will have to use the *shamir** which Moses used for cutting the Precious Stones for the breastplate of the High Priest.'

Said Solomon, 'Where can it be found?'

They said, 'Bring a male and female demon and tie them together. Perhaps they will be able to tell you.'

Solomon was able to do this, as he had power over the demons. So he brought a male and a female demon and tied them together.

They said to him, 'We do not know the whereabouts of the *shamir*, but perhaps Ashmedai, the Prince of the Demons, knows.'

Said Solomon, 'Where is Ashmedai?'

They answered, 'He lives on a mountain to which we can direct you.'

Said Solomon, 'How often does he go there?'

They replied, 'He goes there once a day to drink from his

---

*It is not quite certain what this wonderful stone-splitter was. In post-Talmudic legend, it was a magical worm. Earlier, however, it seems to have been regarded simply as a very hard substance such as diamond or adamant.

49

well. He dug it there himself, and filled it with water, and covered it with a stone, and sealed it with his seal. Every day he goes up to heaven and studies in the Academy of the sky, and then he comes down to earth and studies in the Academy of the earth. Then he visits his mountain and examines his seal to make sure no one has tampered with it. Then he opens the well, drinks water, covers it with the stone, seals it with his seal, and goes away.'

Solomon called to his servant, Benaiahu the son of Jehoiada, the great hero.

Said Solomon, 'Here is a chain engraved with the Name of God, and a ring also engraved with the Name of God, and fleeces of wool, and bottles of wine. Take them with you, and use them as you see fit.'

Benaiahu arrived at the mountain, and found the well covered with a stone and sealed with the seal of Ashmedai. He dug a pit a little lower down the mountain and pierced the floor of the well so that the water flowed out of the well and into the pit. Then he repaired the floor of the well by stuffing the fleeces of wool into the hole he had made in it. Then he dug another pit a little higher up the mountain than the well, and pierced the roof of the well. Then he poured all the wine from the wine-bottles into his pit so that it flowed through into Ashmedai's well. Then he filled up both the pits he had made, so that all seemed exactly as before. Then he went and sat on a tree to wait.

Ashmedai came and examined his seal to see if anyone had tampered with it. Then he opened the well, and found it full of wine instead of water.

Said Ashmedai, 'It is written in Scripture, "Wine taketh away the understanding" [Hosea, 4: 11]. I will not drink it.'

But soon he became so thirsty that he could not resist the wine. He drank it till he became drunk and fell asleep.

Then Benaiahu climbed down from the tree. He took the chain engraved with the Name of God, threw it over Ashmedai, and fastened it. Ashmedai woke up and found himself bound and began to struggle, but Benaiahu said, 'The Name of thy Master is upon thee!' and he stopped struggling.

Benaiahu began to lead the King of the Demons to Solomon. Ashmedai followed obediently in his chains, though his strength was so great that if he happened to brush against a palm-tree or a house, it fell down.

As they went along, Ashmedai saw a wedding procession making its way merrily, and he wept.

Then he heard a man say to a shoemaker, 'Make me a pair of shoes that will last seven years,' and he laughed.

Then he saw a fortune-teller telling fortunes, and he laughed.

Benaiah said to him, 'Why, when you saw the wedding procession, did you weep?'

Said Ashmedai, 'The husband will die within thirty days.'

Benaiahu said, 'Why, when you heard the man say to the shoe-maker, "Make me a pair of shoes that will last seven years," did you laugh?'

Said Ashmedai, 'That man has only seven days to live, and he wants shoes that will last seven years!'

Benaiahu said, 'Why, when you saw the fortune-teller telling fortunes, did you laugh?'

Said Ashmedai, 'In the ground just below where he was sitting was buried a treasure of kings. If he had the gift of fortune-telling, he should have known.'

Finally, they reached Jerusalem, and after three days, Solomon called for him to be brought to his presence.

Ashmedai took a reed and measured four cubits with it on the ground before King Solomon.

'See,' he said, 'despite all your glory, one day you will have only four cubits in this world.'

Then Ashmedai said, 'You have subdued the whole world, yet you are not satisfied until you subdue me.'

Said King Solomon, 'I want nothing of you. It is only that I desire to build the Temple.'

Said Ashmedai, 'Why do you need me to build the Temple?'

Said King Solomon, 'I must have the *shamir*, so that I can cut the stones for the Temple without using iron tools.'

Said Ashmedai, 'It is not in my possession. It is in the possession of the Prince of the Sea, and he trusts it only to the Wild Cock.'

'And what does the Wild Cock do with it?'

'He increases cultivated land with it; for when he comes to a bare mountain, he places the *shamir* on the bare rock, and this causes it to split open and reveal the soil. Then the Wild Cock drops seeds from his mouth into the opened-up soil and trees and vegetation grow.'

They led away Ashmedai, and King Solomon considered how to trick the Wild Cock.

Again he sent his servant Benaiahu. After a long search, Benaiahu found the nest of the Wild Cock, with his young inside it. So Benaiahu placed a thick sheet of glass on top of the nest. Then he hid himself and waited.

Finally, the Wild Cock came, with food for his young. He dropped the food into the nest, but it was stopped by the glass. The Wild Cock tried to enter its nest but could not, so he flew off. After a while, he returned with the *shamir* in his mouth, and placed it on the glass. Suddenly, Benaiahu gave a huge shout. The Wild Cock opened his mouth in surprise, relaxing his grip in the *shamir*, and Benaiahu darted up and snatched it away.

When the Wild Cock saw that he had lost the *shamir*, and betrayed the trust of the Prince of the Sea, he became mournful, and choked himself to death.

Benaiahu returned to King Solomon and brought him the *shamir*, and with it, King Solomon was able to build the Temple without iron tools, for the *shamir* could split the hardest rocks. All the time that he was building the Temple, Solomon kept Ashmedai with him, and often had him brought into his presence, so that he could talk to him, and ask him questions.

One day, after the Temple had been completed, Solomon was sitting alone with Ashmedai. All this time, the chain with with the Name of God had been on Ashmedai's limbs.

Said Solomon, 'What are the special powers that God has given to the demons?'

Said Ashmedai, 'Take the chain off me, and give me your ring, and I will show you.'

So King Solomon took off the chain and gave him the ring.

Then Ashmedai, King of the Demons, placed one wing on the earth and one on the sky, and he seized King Solomon and hurled him into the air so that he landed four hundred parasangs away, in a strange place where no one knew him. And Ashmedai assumed the appearance of King Solomon, and reigned in the palace in his place.

Solomon went begging from place to place, and everywhere he went, he said, 'I, Koheleth, was king over Israel in Jerusalem' [Ecclesiastes, 2: 10]. But no one believed him. Finally, he arrived at Jerusalem and came before the Sanhedrin, claiming to be the King.

The Rabbis of the Sanhedrin tested him in other matters and found him sane, so they began to say among themselves, 'What is the meaning of this?' They sent for Benaiahu, the King's servant and questioned him.

'Does the King send for you lately?'

Said Benaiahu, 'No.'

They then sent an enquiry to the queens in Solomon's harem: 'Does the King visit you lately?'

The queens replied, 'Yes, he does.'

They sent the question, 'Have you noticed anything different about him?'

The queens replied, 'Yes. He always keeps his legs covered. Also, he seeks intercourse with us even when we are menstruating. Also, he even seeks intercourse with Bathsheba, his mother.'

Then the Rabbis contrived to gain possession of the chain and the ring from Ashmedai, and they gave them to Solomon, who took them and entered the palace. When Ashmedai saw Solomon advancing on him with the chain and the ring, he changed to his former shape and flew away.

But Solomon always remained in fear that Ashmedai would return. That is why it is written, 'Sixty warriors guard the bed of Solomon' [Song of Songs, 3: 7].

Gittin, 68b

Note. Although Ashmedai is called King of the Demons, he is not regarded like the Satan or Lucifer of Christian myth. He is not the ruler of a Kingdom of Evil, pitted against God to win the souls of mankind. Ashmedai is more like the djinns of the Arabian Nights. He is mischievous, but also quite genial; and his special powers can sometimes be at the service of man, though his loyalty is always uncertain. He is one of the strange creatures with which the unfathomable universe teems.

Tales of the Rabbis

THE UGLY WIFE

A certain man said to his wife, 'I vow that you will derive no benefit from me until you show me that there is something beautiful in you.'

He came before Rabbi Ishmael ben Rabbi Yosi, who said to him, 'Perhaps her head is beautifully shaped.'

He said to him, 'No, it is round.'

'Perhaps she has beautiful hair.'

'No, it is like stalks of flax.'

'Perhaps her eyes are beautiful.'

'Goggle-eyed.'

'Perhaps her ears are beautiful.'

'They are doubled over.'

'Perhaps her nose is beautiful.'

'It is swollen.'

'Her lips?'

'Thick.'

'Her neck?'

'Sunken.'

'Her belly?'

'Distended.'

'Her legs?'

'She waddles like a goose.'

'Perhaps she has a beautiful name?'

'She is called Muck.'

'The vow is fulfilled. Her name suits her beautifully.'

Nedarim, 66b

A CONVERSATION ON VOWS

MANKOWITZ   Let's discuss this story about the ugly wife and the husband who vowed that she would derive no benefit from him. What does this story demonstrate, apart from the ability of a rabbi to get himself out of trouble when he's asked a complicated question?

MACCOBY   It's connected with the laws of vows. If somebody makes a vow, it's very important, in Judaism, that he should fulfil the vow. But on the other hand it's considered that if he makes a rash vow, then it ought to be brought out that there are consequences of his vow that he never intended; and if it can be shown that when he made the vow he didn't understand some part of the total situation, then the vow can be annulled by a rabbi. It has to be done in this rather official way—he can't just say to himself, 'I never thought of that at the time when I made the vow, so I'm not going to fulfil it.' He has to have a kind of public ceremony in which he is interrogated by a rabbi who has the authority to annul vows, and if the rabbi can find a loophole and show that at the time he made the vow there was some part of the total situation of which he wasn't aware, then the vow can be annulled. As an example of a rash vow, the Talmud cites the case of Jephtha in the Bible. He made a vow that if he was victorious in the war that he was fighting he would sacrifice the first thing that came to meet him on his way home, and it turned out to be his daughter. So he sacrificed his daughter. The rabbis say that this shows that Jephtha didn't understand the theory of vows, because if he'd known it was going to be his daughter, he wouldn't have made the vow. Even though he didn't consciously make an exception of his daughter at the time he made the vow, he unconsciously made that exception and therefore it's the object of the rabbi

	to bring out the unconscious exceptions which are in the mind of the vower.
MANKOWITZ	I think that's very good. The example shows that there are humane considerations below the apparently totally rational level of a person's statements. 'I will kill the first thing I meet. The first thing is my daughter. I kill my daughter.' that is the rational statement. In life there is a whole infrastructure of unconscious meaning and reference. Now if you are saying that the rabbinical, the Talmudical explanation is intended to bring out the infrastructure and to humanize men's purely rational and frequently cruel and thoughtless feelings and behaviour which nevertheless is undeniably rational, then I see the point. It does seem to me that the essence of this story about the man and his wife lies in this: here is this man with this incredibly ugly, unattractive wife, and he is really trying to exploit the laws of vows in order to ill-treat this unfortunate woman who nevertheless is his wife. So he says to her, 'I vow'—which, as a religious Jew, commits him to fulfil what he's going to say—'that you will derive no benefit from me until you show me that there is something beautiful in you.' He is trying to twist the essence of the process of vowing and to exploit and manipulate it against his wife. He is saying, in effect, 'I am not going to give you anything, whatever happens, because we all know there is nothing beautiful in you.' And yet, as a result of this exchange, Rabbi Ishmael is able to demonstrate that there is a humane interpretation of the situation which will justify and support the woman. So the law of vows is supportive to the weak. That is how it appears to me.
MACCOBY	Perhaps you are being a little too hard on the husband. After all, he did come to Rabbi Ishmael and ask to have his vow annulled. Somehow or other, despite the fact that his wife was

so without beauty, he wanted to go back on his vow, which amounted to a severance of relations with her. Perhaps he was really good-hearted, and made his vow in a moment of irritation of which he repented. Of course, the story is exaggerated—it probably never happened—it's just a piece of fiction, but an interesting one. The Talmud likes to push an idea to its extreme limit, and you need imagination to do that.

MANKOWITZ   The writer is an excellent dialogue writer. But doesn't this story show that a promise, in Talmudic law, is not binding, and you can get out of it by having it annulled?

MACCOBY   That is an important point to answer, because anti-Semites have often fastened on this aspect of the Talmud, which they have interpreted to mean, 'You can't trust the word of a Jew, because he can always go to his rabbi and get out of it.'

MANKOWITZ   So we come back to my first question. Is this just a clever method of evasion by the rabbis?

MACCOBY   The first point to stress is that a vow is a very different thing from a promise. This law applies to vows, not to promises, or contracts. You can't get out of a business contract, for example, either a written one or a verbal one, by saying, 'At the time that I made this contract, I didn't realize that such and such would be the consequence.' The answer to that is, 'You should have thought of that at the time that you made the contract.' The only thing you can get out of is a vow, which is an undertaking made between a man and himself, not between a man and his neighbour. A second point is this: although the rabbis exercised their ingenuity on vows—some of the most brilliant examples of ingenuity in the Talmud are in this area—at the same time, they set their faces against making it into simply an intellectual exercise. There were many occasions when they refused to absolve people

57

from vows, because they said, 'You understood perfectly well what you were saying at the time you made your vow.' And the very fact that a ceremony of absolution, after a pretty strict enquiry, is necessary, shows how seriously they took vows. After all, the Torah says that if a man makes a vow, 'he shall do according to all that proceedeth out of his mouth'; once those words come out of his mouth, they cannot be shrugged off. At the same time, the Talmud would really prefer that people should not make vows at all—there are several passages in the Talmud to this effect. There's a corresponding passage, if you remember, in the New Testament: 'Let your speech be Yea, yea, Nay, nay.' Yet once a vow had been made, it became a fact, and something had to be done about it. Another point that might be mentioned here is the question of the *Kol Nidrei** passage in the Day of Atonement service. This is often brought up in anti-Semitic literature. The *Kol Nidrei* declaration is a cancellation of vows, and appears to say, 'All the vows that I am about to make in the coming year are hereby cancelled.' So of course, the anti-Semitic reaction is, 'How can you trust the word of a Jew, when he cancels all his obligations in advance?' Again, the point is that *Kol Nidrei* refers only to vows—restrictions which a man lays on himself—not to contractual obligations to other people.

MANKOWITZ   So it's between him and God?

MACCOBY   Yes. The original form of the *Kol Nidrei* did not refer to the future, but to the past. What it really meant was, 'If I've made any resolutions which I've forgotten about'—again we come to the unconscious aspect which we discussed before—'I

*This expression means 'All Vows . . .' and forms the first words of the declaration, annulling vows, which opens the evening service at the start of the Day of Atonement.

58

hereby disavow them.' It's like a man on his death-bed, tying up the loose ends of his life. Yom Kippur (the Day of Atonement) is like a death, followed by a resurrection. It is natural, then, that facing one's death, one says, 'I hereby cancel all the resolutions which I have failed to fulfil.' Even that, however, was not approved by the rabbis. The *Kol Nidrei* declaration was banned by the rabbis of Babylonia, the Geonim, who succeeded the rabbis who figure in the Talmud. They said, 'We don't make this declaration here, and we don't approve of it.' They tried to stop it, but failed. This was a folk custom which got such a psychological hold over the Jewish people that in the end the rabbis had to acquiesce in it. The psychoanalyst Karl Abraham wrote an interesting article about this.

MANKOWITZ So this apparently humorous little story provides a basis for a full discussion of the ethics of vow-making, and how it differs and relates to bond-making. Some extremely important and complex ethical questions are contained within quite humorous and highly-animated tableaux in the Talmud—I think this exemplifies that point.

WHEN RABBAH GOT DRUNK

Said Rava, 'A man ought to get so drunk on Purim that he cannot distinguish between "Cursed is Haman" and "Blessed is Mordechai".'

Rabbah and Rabbi Zeira once made a Purim feast together. They got drunk, and Rabbah rose up and cut Rabbi Zeira's throat. In the morning, Rabbah prayed to God, and brought Rabbi Zeira to life again.

Next year, Rabbah invited Rabbi Zeira to join him for a Purim feast again.

'No, thank you,' said Rabbi Zeira. 'A miracle may not happen every time.'

Megillah, 7b

Once Rabbi Ishmael ben Rabbi Yose was going on the road when he met a certain man who was carrying a load of sticks. The man put down the bundles of sticks to have a rest. Said the man to Rabbi Ishmael, 'Load me up' [in accordance with the Biblical commandment, Exodus, 23: 5].

Said Rabbi Ishmael (who was very fat, and also rich), 'How much are the sticks worth?'

'Half a zuz.'

Rabbi Ishmael paid the man half a zuz, and said, 'I declare these sticks ownerless.'

Said the man, 'I claim ownership of these ownerless sticks. Now'—(to Rabbi Ishmael)—'load me up.'

Rabbi Ishmael gave him another half-zuz, and declared the sticks ownerless again. He saw that the man was about to claim ownership again, so he said, 'To all the world except you I have declared them ownerless.'

But can one declare a thing ownerless with such a condition? Have we not learnt from the Mishnah that a declaration of ownerlessness is always unconditional? The answer is that Rabbi Ishmael's declaration was unconditional, but he used a form of words to circumvent the man.

Bava Metsia, 30b

Note. Why did R. Ishmael have to declare the sticks ownerless? Why not simply go on his way? The answer is that the sticks would then have been his possession, and any wayfarer who took them would have incurred the sin of theft. Another saintly Rabbi, when he saw a thief making off with his possessions, shouted out 'Hefker!' ('Ownerless!') so that the sin of theft would be removed from the would-be thief.

WERE THE LIONS HUNGRY?

Caesar said to Rabbi Tanhum, 'Come, let us all become one people.'

Said Rabbi Tanhum, 'By my life, we who are circumcised cannot become like you. You, then, should be circumcised and become like us.'

'A very good answer. Unfortunately, however, anyone who defeats the Emperor in an argument must be thrown to the lions.'

So they threw Rabbi Tanhum to the lions. The lions, however, did not eat him.

An unbeliever, who was standing by, said, 'The reason why the lions do not eat him is that they are not hungry.'

To test this theory, they threw the unbeliever to the lions, who ate him.

Sanhedrin, 39a

THE RAINMAKER

Abba Hilkiah was the grandson of Honi the Circle-maker; and when the world needed rain, the Rabbis used to send a delegation to him, and he would pray for rain, and it would come.

Once the world needed rain. The Rabbis sent a pair of rabbis to him to pray for mercy that rain might come. They went to his house and did not find him there. They went into the fields, and found him hoeing. They greeted him with 'Peace', but he did not turn his face to them. In the evening, when he had collected some twigs, he set out for home, carrying the twigs and the hoe on one shoulder, and his cloak on the other shoulder.

All the journey he walked barefoot, but when he came to water, he put on his shoes.

When he came to prickly shrubs and brambles, he lifted up his clothes.

When he reached his house, his wife came out to meet him, adorned with ornaments.

His wife went in first, then he went in, and the rabbis went in last.

He sat down to eat, and did not say to the rabbis, 'Come, eat with us.'

He divided the bread for his children, giving one portion to the elder and two portions to the younger.

Then he said to his wife, 'I know that the rabbis have come about rain. Let us go up to the roof and pray for mercy. Perhaps the Holy One, blessed be He, will be pleased to send rain, without any credit being given to us.'

They went up to the roof. He stood at one corner of the roof and prayed, and she stood at the opposite corner and prayed. When the rain-clouds appeared, they came first from the direction of her corner.

When he descended from the roof, he turned to the rabbis and said, 'Why have the rabbis come?'

They said, 'The Rabbis sent us to the Master, that he might ask mercy for rain.'

He said to them, 'Blessed be the All-present, who has made it unnecessary for you to call on the services of Abba Hilkiah.'

They said to him, 'We know that the rain came because of the Master. But let the Master tell us these things, at which we wonder: why, when we greeted the Master with "Peace", did he not turn his face to us?'

He said to them, 'I was hired for the day, and I thought I should not spend any of the time in idleness.'

'And why did the Master carry the twigs on one shoulder and the cloak on the other?'

He said to them, 'It was a borrowed garment. It was lent to act as a cloak, not to carry twigs on it.'

'Why did the Master walk all the journey without shoes, but put them on when he came to water?'

He said to them, 'All the journey I could see what lay before me, but in the water I could not see what lay before me.'

'Why, when the Master came to prickly shrubs or brambles, did he lift up his clothes?'

'Because flesh heals but clothes do not heal.'

'Why, when the Master reached his house, did the wife of the Master come out adorned with ornaments?'

He said to them, 'So that I would not put my eyes on another woman.'

'Why did she go in first, then the Master after her, and we last of all?'

He said to them, 'Because you are not well known to me.'

'Why, when the Master began to eat, did he not invite us to eat?'

'Because there was not much food, and you would have refrained politely from eating, and I did not want the credit of doing you a favour which was in fact no favour.'

'Why did the Master give his elder child one portion of bread, and his younger child two?'

'The elder son stays in the house, and the younger stays all day in the school (where he is not given a meal).'

'And why did the rain-clouds come first from the direction of the corner where the Master's wife was standing?'

'Because she is always in the house and gives bread to the poor who come to the house, and the enjoyment of bread is immediate; while I give money, the enjoyment of which is not immediate. Or perhaps it is because of the bandits who were in our neighbourhood; I prayed to God that they should die, but she prayed that they should repent.'

Ta'anit, 23a

THE JEWISH RIP VAN WINKLE

One day, Honi the Circle-maker was going on the road when he saw a man who was planting a carob-tree.

Said Honi to the man, 'How many years will it be before this tree bears fruit?'

Said the man, 'Seventy years.'

Said Honi, 'Do you think you will live another seventy years?'

Said the man, 'Just as I have found carob-trees which my ancestors planted for me, so I plant carob-trees for my descendants.'

Honi sat down and started to eat his meal. Then a deep sleep came over him. A cave formed itself round him and hid him from the eyes of men. And he slept on for seventy years.

When he went out, he came across a man standing by the carob-tree and gathering fruit from it.

Said Honi, 'Are you the man who planted this tree?'

'No,' said the man. 'I am his grand-son.'

He went to his house and asked the people there, 'Is the son of Honi the Circle-maker still alive?'

'No,' they said. 'His son has died, but his grandson is alive.'

He said to them, 'I am Honi the Circle-maker.' But they did not believe him.

He went to the House of Learning. There he heard one of the

63

Rabbis talking. 'This argument is as clear as in the days of Honi the Circle-maker, in whose days no difficulty remained unsolved, for when Honi entered the House of Learning he answered all the perplexities of the Rabbis.'

Said he, 'I am Honi the Circle-maker.' But they did not believe him. Nor did they give him the honour which was his due. He became distressed and prayed for death, and God answered his prayer.

Commented Rava, 'This is as men say, "Either comradeship, or death." '

Ta'anit, 23a

Note. What gives this story depth is the introductory part about the planting of the carob-tree. Honi, the great scholar, does not understand what the simple peasant understands; that the work is not for oneself, but for the race, and that a man ripens and dies like a plant.

THE GOLDEN LEG

Rabbi Hanina ben Dosa was very poor. One day, his wife said to him, 'How long must we suffer like this?'

Said he, 'What shall we do?'

Said she, 'Pray that you may be given something.'

He prayed, and a hand appeared which gave him one leg of a golden table.

That night he dreamt that he heard a voice saying, 'In the World to Come, the righteous will eat at tables with three legs, but you will eat at a table with only two legs.'

He told this to his wife, and she said, 'Are you content that everyone else should eat at a three-legged table, and we should eat at a two-legged table?'

Said he, 'What shall we do?'

Said she, 'Pray that the golden leg should be taken back again.'

He prayed, and the golden leg was taken back.

It was taught: the second miracle was greater than the first.

Ta'anit, 25a

THE SNAKE IT WAS THAT DIED

While Rabbi Hanina ben Dosa was praying, a snake bit him, but he continued his prayer without interruption. Later, the snake was found dead at the entrance to its hole, while Rabbi Hanina showed no ill effects.

From this arose the saying, 'Woe to the man who is bitten by a snake, and woe to the snake that has bitten Rabbi Hanina ben Dosa!'

Palestinian Talmud, Berakhot, 9a

TWO KINDS OF RABBI

It once happened that Rabbi Hanina ben Dosa went to learn Torah with Rabban Johanan ben Zakkai, and Rabban Johanan's son fell ill.

Said Rabban Johanan, 'Hanina, my son, pray for him that he may live.'

Rabbi Hanina put his head between his knees and prayed; and the son recovered.

Said Rabban Johanan ben Zakkai, 'If the son of Zakkai had banged his head between his knees all day long, there would have been no result.'

His wife said to him, 'And is Hanina a greater man than you?'

He said to her, 'No; but he is like a favourite slave before the king, and I am like a prince before the king.'

Berakhot, 34b

Note. Some scholars have interpreted this story as evidence of rivalry and bad blood between Rabban Johanan ben Zakkai and Rabbi Hanina ben Dosa; or, in a more general way, between 'legalistic' rabbis and 'charismatic' rabbis. This is a very superficial way to understand the story. Note the humility with which the great Johanan ben Zakkai admits that his powers of prayer are far inferior to those of Hanina ben Dosa—the self-depreciatory humour with which he imagines himself banging his head in an endeavour to equal Hanina (he calls himself 'the son of Zakkai', which is a depreciatory idiom). Yet, paradoxically, he then asserts with pride his high status as a prince before God, as

65

compared with Hanina, who is only a palace slave, whose whims the king humours, like a spoilt child.

Expressed here is a two-fold approach to God, both sides of which are valid in their different ways. There is the approach of intimacy and nearness to God, resulting in miracle-working and charisma; and the approach of dignity and rationality, the covenant-relationship in which man enters into friendship with God rather than child-like dependence.

COMMERCIAL USES OF A SAINT

Rav Huna kept barrels of wine in a house which, as it turned out, was in danger of collapsing, so he wished to remove the wine from there before the house collapsed.

He persuaded Rav Aha bar Ahavah to use the house for his studies, being quite sure that as long as that saintly man was in the house, it would not collapse. This gave him time to remove all the barrels of wine, but when, after that, Rav Aha bar Ahavah left the house, it immediately fell down.

Rav Aha bar Ahavah noticed what had happened and guessed what Rav Huna had done. He was very annoyed, because he agreed with the saying of Rabbi Yannai: 'A man should never stand in a place of danger and say, "A miracle will be done for me." Perhaps a miracle will not be done for him, and if it is done, his merits will be lessened.'

Ta'anit, 20b

THE PROSTITUTE'S FART

It was said of Rabbi Eleazar ben Dordai that he did not omit having intercourse with any prostitute in the world. Once he heard that there was a certain prostitute in a sea-port who accepted a purse of denarii for payment. So he took a purse of denarii, and he crossed seven rivers to reach her.

As he was beginning intercourse with her, she farted. Upon this, she commented, 'Just as this fart will never return to its place, so Eleazar ben Dordai will never return to God and be accepted.'

He went and sat between two mountain-ranges, and said, 'Mountain-ranges, plead with God to have mercy on me.'

Said the mountain-ranges, 'Before we pray for you, we should pray for ourselves, for Scripture says, "For the mountains shall depart and the hills be removed" [Isaiah, 54: 10].'

He said, 'Heavens and Earth, ask God to have mercy on me.'

Said the Heavens and Earth, 'Before we pray for you, we should pray for ourselves, for Scripture says, "For the heavens shall vanish away like smoke, and the earth shall wax old like a garment" [Isaiah, 51: 6].'

He said, 'Sun and Moon, ask God to have mercy on me.'

Said the Sun and Moon, 'Before we pray for you, we should pray for ourselves, for Scripture says, "Then the moon shall be confounded and the sun ashamed" [Isaiah, 24: 23].'

He said, 'Stars and Constellations, ask God for mercy on me.'

Said the Stars and Constellations, 'Before we pray for you, we should pray for ourselves, for Scripture says, "And all the hosts of heaven shall moulder away" [Isaiah, 34: 4].'

He said, 'Then the thing depends on me alone.' He put his head between his knees, and groaned and wept until his soul departed.

Then a heavenly voice went forth and said, 'Rabbi Eleazar ben Dordai has been summoned to the life of the World to Come.'

Rabbi Judah the Prince, when he heard of this, wept, and said, 'There are those who gain the World to Come by the toil of many years; and there are those who gain the World to Come in one hour.'

And he added, 'It is not enough for those who repent that they are accepted; they are called "Rabbi" too!'

Avodah Zarah, 17a

Note. The first part of this story has been bowdlerized out of recognition in the Soncino Talmud and other translations. These versions censor out the fart altogether. But the whole point is to show how small a thing can set a man on the road to repentance —even a prostitute's fart. A parallel story in the Gospels is the parable of the labourers in the vineyard, where those who laboured in the heat of the day are annoyed because those who started work in the last hour are paid the same wage.

Parables

THE LAME MAN AND THE BLIND MAN

The Emperor Antoninus said to Rabbi Judah the Prince, 'On the Day of Judgment, the body and the soul can both plead innocence. The body can plead, "Without the soul I am blind and dumb." The soul can plead, "Without the body, I am helpless." '

Said Rabbi Judah the Prince, 'I will tell you a parable. A king owned a beautiful orchard which contained fine figs. He appointed two watchmen therein, one lame and the other blind. One day, the lame man said to the blind man, "I see beautiful figs in the orchard. Come and take me upon your shoulder, so that we may get hold of them and eat them." So the lame man climbed onto the blind man, reached the fruit and they both ate it. Some time after, the owner of the orchard came and asked, "Where are my figs?" The lame man replied, "Have I feet to walk with?" The blind man replied, "Have I eyes to see with?" What did the king do? He placed the lame man on the shoulders of the blind man, and judged them together. So the Holy One, blessed be He, will bring the soul, replace it in the body, and judge them together.'

Sanhedrin, 91a

THE FLOWER

A certain king had a garden, in which were planted rows of fig trees, vines, pomegranates and apples. He entrusted it to a tenant-farmer and went away. After a time, the king returned,

68

and looking into the garden to know what it had produced, found it full of thorns and thistles. So he brought in wood-cutters to destroy the garden utterly. But as he looked among the thorns, he noticed a single rose-coloured flower. He took it, and smelt it, and his spirit found rest in it.

Said the king, 'For the sake of this flower, the whole garden will be saved.'

Leviticus Rabbah, 23: 3

THE FOX

Once a fox found a vineyard which was fenced round on all sides, but had one little hole in it. What did he do? He fasted three days until he became thin and weak, and then he entered through the hole into the vineyard. There he ate and grew fat, but when he wanted to go out, he was unable to get through the hole again. So once more he fasted for three days until he was thin and weak, just as he was before, and so went out. When he was out, he turned his face towards the vineyard and said, 'Vineyard, vineyard, how good is your fruit! Everything in you is beautiful and worthy of praise. But what profit is there from you? Just as one enters you, so one must go out.'

So said the Preacher, 'As he came forth from his mother's womb, naked shall he go back as he came, and shall take nothing for his labour' [Ecclesiastes, 5: 14].

Ecclesiastes Rabbah, 5: 14

THE KING'S GARDEN

Said Rabbi Simeon ben Halafta, 'Someone who has learnt the words of the Law and does not fulfil them, is more deserving of punishment than someone who has never learnt them at all.

'To what shall the matter be likened? To a king, who possessed a garden. He leased it to two tenant-farmers. One of them did not plant any trees at all. The other planted trees, and then chopped them down. With whom was the king angry?

69

Was it not with the one who planted trees and then chopped them down?'

Deuteronomy Rabbah, 7: 4

THE KING AND THE STAG

A king had a flock which went out to the fields, and came in again in the evening. So it was every day. One day a stag came in with the flock. He went along with the goats and grazed with them. The king was told, 'A stag has joined the flock and is grazing with them every day, going out with them and coming in with them.' The king felt love for the stag, and when he saw him going out to the fields, he gave orders, 'Let him have good pasture according to his will: no man shall beat him; take great care with him!' And also when the stag came in with the flock, the king would say, 'Give him to drink.' So he showed that he loved him very much.

The king's servants said to him, 'My lord, how many rams are yours, how many sheep are yours, how many goats are yours, yet you give us no special instructions concerning them. Yet about this stag, every day you give us your commands.'

Said the king to them, 'The flock, whether they want to or not, thus is their way, to graze in the field every day, and in the evening to come in to sleep in the fold. The stags sleep in the wilderness; it is not their way to enter the places cultivated by men. Shall we not then account it as a merit to this one who has left behind the whole of the broad, vast wilderness, the abode of all the beasts, and has come to stay in the courtyard?'

So God has told us, 'Love ye therefore the proselyte' [Deuteronomy, 10: 19].

Numbers Rabbah, 8: 2

MY PART OF THE SHIP

Some people were once sitting in a ship. One of them took a gimlet and began to bore a hole in the ship in the part under where he was sitting.

His comrades said to him, 'What are you sitting and doing?'

He said to them, 'What has it to do with you? Am I not boring a hole in my part of the ship?'

They said to him, 'But the water is coming in and sinking the ship under us.'

So it is with Israel. One sins and all are affected.

Leviticus Rabbah, 4: 5

A CONVERSATION ON JEWISH PARTICULARISM

MANKOWITZ   Let's talk about this parable about the man who bored a hole in his own part of the ship, and then felt surprised when other people on the ship began to object. What do you feel about this, Hyam?

MACCOBY   This is more the kind of moral tale that you find in the usual anthology—I included it because there is a certain element of humour in it. But really it's just quite a banal moral tale about how one's actions never affect just oneself alone, they affect everybody else. Even if you are doing something which you imagine is simply your own business, it never is just your own business, because you are a member of a community. One other point—this is a good example of the genre of parables—the Talmud is very fond of parables, little stories which illustrate a point, but sometimes take off into an imaginative world of their own and become works of art. The parables of Jesus in the Gospels are very much part of this Talmudic genre.

MANKOWITZ   This story could be invoked in relation to the revival of the anti-Zionist, anti-Jewish syndrome that's heavily under discussion at the moment.

MACCOBY   How does it tie up?

MANKOWITZ   Because of the implication of solidarity—all Jews are in the same boat.

MACCOBY   Yes, I see.

MANKOWITZ   The boat flies a flag. If the flag is pale blue with a white Magen David on it, then the Jews are Zionists.

71

MACCOBY	Because the Jews have solidarity and feel themselves to be a community, this is interpreted by people as being exclusive: 'Those Jews always hang together.'
MANKOWITZ	I think we might discuss the question, 'How can one be a Jew, and keep one's loyalty to the society in which one lives?'
MACCOBY	Yes, the parable we are discussing gives its moral as: 'And so it is with Israel . . .' It doesn't refer the moral to the whole world. Why doesn't the boat include everybody in the world, not just the people Israel? I would say that Judaism *is* a universal religion, but it is not a universal Church. This is one important difference between Judaism and Christianity. Christianity is both a universal religion and a universal Church—everybody in the world, in principle, must belong to Christendom. The Jews worship the One God who created heaven and earth, but they themselves are just one nation, and they don't expect everybody in the world to be Jews. They expect every nation to have its own national loyalties and to worship God in their own way. And they don't require other nations to become part of the Jewish church, because the Jewish church is a national church. Even though there has been a certain amount of missionary activity among Jews—there have been some very great missionary periods—there has never been a desperate feeling that everybody in the world must become Jews, or otherwise they will be damned and all go to hell.
MANKOWITZ	The Jew concedes the right to separateness.
MACCOBY	Yes, and because he concedes the separateness of Greece, or of England, or of Germany, he can glory in the separateness of being a Jew as well. That doesn't mean that by doing so he's being exclusive—on the contrary, he's showing more respect for the other person's nationality just because he's glorying in his own nationality.
MANKOWTIZ	So this is really a case of devolved regionalists?

MACCOBY	Quite so, a regionalist religion. It's universalist and yet it's particularist at the same time.
MANKOWITZ	But what exactly is the status of those Gentiles who do become converted to Judaism? After all, as we know, quite a high proportion of Jews today are descended from converts of every possible nation and race. According to Arthur Koestler in his recent book on the Khazar Empire, which became converted to Judaism in the Dark Ages, most Jews today are actually descended from these Khazars, who were of Turkish race. This, no doubt, is an exaggerated thesis, but it remains true that the original Semitic stock of the Jews has been adulterated out of recognition in the millennia of Jewish history. To mention only one source of adulteration, we know that countless Jewish women were raped in the course of Gentile persecutions, and every child born in this way was brought up as a Jew and treated as a full Jew in every way. Similarly, every convert to Judaism is a full Jew. What exactly is the meaning of such conversion, if Judaism is as regionalist as you have made out?
MACCOBY	All that you have said is perfectly true, but what it means is simply that the Jews are a nation and not a race or tribe. The Jews have never felt the slightest concern for their racial purity. Anyone who wishes to become a Jew can do so, by adopting the Jewish way of worshipping God. It is something like becoming a naturalized Englishman, but even more like joining some religious order, except that it is an intermarrying religious order, which vows to marry only another member of the order. Those who feel a vocation to leave the nation of their birth and join the religious communion of the Jewish nation, are welcomed, but there is no obligation to perform such a sacrifice. All that is required of the great majority of mankind is to worship the One God and to observe the basic rules of human decency

73

	as laid down in the code called the Laws of the Sons of Noah,* the first code of international law ever promulgated, which can be found in the Talmud.
MANKOWITZ	To return to our parable, isn't there another aspect, that of 'Don't make trouble'? If you're a Jew, you've got to be on special behaviour—if you behave badly in school, everybody is going to say, 'Jews are like that.'
MACCOBY	Yes, I think so. That kind of parable is more likely to arise in times of trouble. The image of the boat is an image of danger. But I would prefer not to take it that way. I would prefer to take the boat as an image of society in general, of which 'Israel' is only a special case. Even if society is not under any special outside threat, it is still a fabric which depends on the actions of every individual. I like the image of the boat because it combines two things which Judaism does combine, individualism and community-feeling. Society is indivisible, but it depends on the actions of the individual. I think this parable has more in it than I realized at first.

---

*'The Sons of Noah' means the whole of mankind, since Noah was not a Jew but the progenitor of all mankind, Gentiles and Jews. Gentiles are required by Judaism to keep the Seven Laws, which are the basic rules of morality. The special laws obligatory for Jews (for example, observance of the Sabbath and of the dietary laws) are not regarded as basic moral laws, and are therefore not obligatory for Gentiles, unless they choose voluntarily to become full Jews. The seventeenth-century founders of international law, Hugo Grotius of Holland, and John Selden of England, took their main inspiration from the Talmudic Seven Laws of the Sons of Noah. See Shabtai Rosenne, 'The Influence of Judaism on the Development of International Law' (*Netherlands International Law Review*, 1958). For the Seven Laws, and their provision for kindness to animals, see p. 172.

MEN AND WOMEN

He who has no wife lives without joy, without blessing, and without good.

Yevamot, 62b

A man should always be careful to honour his wife, for no blessing is found within a man's house except for the sake of his wife.

Bava Metsia, 59a

A man should always take care not to distress his wife, for women's tears are close to the heart of God.

Bava Metsia, 59a

The Holy One, blessed be He, gave greater understanding to women than to men.

Niddah, 45b

Said Rav Hanan, the son of Rav: 'Everybody knows why the bride is brought into the bridal chamber, but if anyone speaks obscenely about it, even if seventy years of happiness have been decreed and sealed for him on High, the decree is changed for him into evil.'

Ketuvot, 8b

Duties of a Husband

These are the rights and duties of a husband towards his wife:

Rights:
1. He is entitled to anything that she finds.
2. He is entitled to her handiwork.
3. He has the right to annul her vows (under certain circumstances).
4. He is entitled to the income from her property.

Duties:
1. He must maintain her, including the provision of suitable clothing and adornments. including cosmetics.
2. He must ransom her, if she is captured.
3. He must provide for her burial. (Rabbi Judah ruled: 'Even the poorest man in Israel must provide no less that two flutes and one lamenting woman.')
4. He must perform his conjugal duty of intercourse with a frequency suitable to his position in life.
(If the husband fails to perform any of these duties, the wife is entitled to divorce, and in case of divorce, the husband must hand over the wife's property in full.)

Some other points:
No adult woman may be forced to marry against her will. If a forced marriage takes place, it is invalid.

A minor may be given in marriage by her father, but when she reaches adulthood, she has the right of 'refusal' [*minui*], and,

78

if she exercises this right, the marriage becomes null and void.

If a wife enters marriage with a dowry, this continues to be her property, and must be returned to her in the event of a divorce. If a wife has no dowry, the husband must pay her two hundred zuzim, a considerable sum, in the event of divorce.

Wife-beating is forbidden. It is regarded as a case of common assault, and a civil action may be brought by the wife against the husband for damages in such a case. A wife is not a chattel or a servant, but an independent citizen who has the same rights in relation to her husband as any other citizen. [Medieval rabbis stated that wife-beating is *worse* than common assault, since the wife is in a vulnerable position. However, wife-beating never became a problem, as it was almost unheard-of. 'This is something not done in Israel,' says one medieval authority.]

Ketuvot, 47b (summary)

THE DUTY OF ONAH

The *Onah* [duty of regular intercourse] mentioned in the Torah [Exodus, 21: 10] is as follows:
  people who do not need to work for a living—every day;
  labourers—twice a week;
  ass-drivers—once a week;
  camel-drivers—once every thirty days;
  sailors—once every six months.
The words of Rabbi Eliezer.

Commentary of Rabbi Obadiah of Bertinoro:
Someone who was originally employed in a trade near his home and wished to change to a trade in which he would have to travel far from home—his wife may prevent him from changing, on the ground that this would make his Onah more infrequent. The exception is the Scholar (whose Onah is once a week on the Sabbath); for if he wished to change from being a non-worker or a labourer to being a Scholar, his wife may not prevent him, even though this would make his Onah more infrequent.

Mishnah, Ketuvot, 5: 6

79

CONVERSATION ON THE DUTY OF A HUSBAND

MANKOWITZ   Every day for people who do not work for a living, twice a week for labourers, once a week for ass drivers, camel drivers once every thirty days, sailors, every six months. It certainly is an extraordinarily specific and definite allocation. Quite clearly there must be a great deal of reasoning and argument and discussion about it—but why, for example, do ass drivers have a greater allocation than a camel driver? I mean, a camel driver may be very much stronger in regard to intercourse than an ass driver.

MACCOBY   This is not a rule for how many times intercourse should take place—it's a minimum. Actually, the more intercourse takes place the better. But intercourse is regarded by the Talmud as a duty that a husband owes to his wife. And a man who is away from home a good deal, or a man who comes home very tired from hard work, can't be expected to perform this duty quite so frequently as someone who has an easier life. That is why a person who has no regular employment at all has no excuse whatever; he must perform his duty every day—that is the minimum for him. But take a camel driver who goes away on long journeys—on caravan journeys to distant places —if you laid down to him that he must have intercourse with his wife every day, then he'd have to come back from his caravan journey before he completed his business; and a sailor might be away for six months on a voyage.

MANKOWITZ   That is accepted, that is extremely reasonable. So, in effect, camel drivers who would like to go on much longer journeys are hereby instructed that they must be home at least once every thirty days, otherwise they're in breach of the law.

MACCOBY   Yes. An ass driver must not say, 'I'm so busy with my work that I can only come back once in six months.' That's a good excuse for a sailor, but not for an ass driver.

MANKOWITZ   Let's consider further, then, how behind this schedule there is the assumption that all men, whether they work for a living or are labourers, ass drivers, camel drivers or sailors, have equal sexual potency. Surely we know from experience that men vary in potency.

MACCOBY   That is quite true, and if a wife, which is quite possible, complained to her rabbi, 'My husband is a camel driver, and is supposed to give me my intercourse once a month, and has failed to do so, only once every two months,' then the rabbi summoned him and said, 'What's the matter, what's the idea? You're failing to fulfil the law. If you don't fulfil the law, you are liable to a punishment.'

MANKOWITZ   What kind of punishment?

MACCOBY   A fine.

MANKOWITZ   So you could be taxed for not making love?

MACCOBY   Certainly, because a man who marries a woman is under an obligation to fulfil his marital duties. The same applies to the woman as well, but it is particularly an obligation for the man, rather than the woman, for several reasons. One reason is polygamy, which however had more or less lapsed by Talmudic times—no rabbi that we know of had more than one wife. Still polygamy was in fact allowed, and still is in Jewish law—*

MANKOWITZ   That's what I keep telling my wife!

MACCOBY   Consequently the wife needed protection in this respect more than the husband. Since a wife is strictly forbidden to have intercourse outside her marriage while a husband is not, she must be compensated by having a law of this kind to protect her rights. But the answer to the point that you made about impotence or lack of potency would be simply this: if a man, having been summoned by the rabbi at the instance of

*European Jews were forbidden polygamy by the Edict of Rabbenu Gershom (c. 1000). Israel has adopted this rule.

the wife for failing to fulfil his duty, has a reasonable excuse, which is his physical deficiency, then of course, just as in the case of any other law, special circumstances can lead to a dispensation.

MANKOWITZ   And supposing there is an ass driver who just isn't fulfilling his marital duty with the required frequency, and his wife goes to the rabbi and complains, and the rabbi discusses the question with the ass driver, and it emerges that the ass driver is not very strong, or whatever reason it is, are there grounds therein for the wife to get a divorce?

MACCOBY   Certainly. This is one of the chief grounds that a wife has for divorce. It could be that the husband has a good excuse on physical grounds, but that doesn't mean that the wife has got to put up with it, though she may choose to do so of her own good will. She can have a divorce if her Onah isn't fulfilled according to the law.

MANKOWITZ   Now supposing I am someone who doesn't work for a living and I haven't worked for a living from, say, the age of 25, when I might reasonably be expected to be very happy and capable of giving my wife or wives their Onah every day. But at, say, 55, am I still required to give all my wives their Onah once a day?

MACCOBY   That's a very good question. I shall have to look up some medieval commentary on that.* I would say that it's a question for assessment. If a man of 55 is not able to perform his duty according to law, then perhaps his wife, out of her graciousness, would be prepared to forgive him. But in fact it is still his duty. There is one of the Psalms which is a very lugubrious, depressed kind of Psalm in which King David is bewailing his lot and saying how weary and full of sorrow and

*The medieval commentary and code, the *Tur*, says: 'The obligation to perform Onah every night for an unoccupied man applies only if he is in perfect health and is free from anxiety, and if he does not have to pay taxes.'

82

trouble he is, and the Talmudic comment on this Psalm is that the reason why he was wailing in that way was that he had eighteen wives, and, being a very pious man, he felt that he had to fulfil his duty according to the law by all eighteen wives, and this was rather taking it out of him.

MANKOWITZ   Every day?

MACCOBY   No, King David was not a man without occupation, he was a very busy man.

MANKOWITZ   Does the wife have any obligations in this matter?

MACCOBY   Yes, the law about a woman is this: if she refuses sexual intercourse to her husband without reasonable excuse—obviously if she is ill, or something like that, that's different—then the husband is entitled to punish his wife by taking a fine from her property. This is something which is quite different from English law, in which any money which the wife brings into the marriage belongs automatically to the husband—or rather this was English law until quite recently. In Jewish law, a wife's money always belongs to her, so it is available, on occasion, for the payment of fines. The husband is entitled to deduct from the wife's money a certain sum which is laid down in the Mishnah, so many *denars* per week, as long as she refuses, until she has no money left, when he is entitled to divorce her.

MANKOWITZ   There seems to be a general idea that in the Jewish tradition, woman has no place except in the home, and as a kind of chattel, and has no rights.

MACCOBY   This, of course, is quite wrong. A Jewish wife has a right of divorce if her husband ill-treats her. This does not mean only gross ill-treatment, such as wife-beating. In most countries, until very recently, wife-beating was regarded as a husband's right—even his duty. In Judaism it was always regarded simply as a case of common assault, only worse, because of the vulnerable position of the wife, who should be under the husband's special protection. That a Jewish wife has a right to divorce if her husband beats her goes without saying—but there are many other less crude forms of ill-treatment which entitle her to a divorce. For example, if her husband takes on a profession which makes him smelly, such as being a tanner, or a coppersmith, or working at a cesspool, she is entitled to divorce her husband for that reason. Or if her husband insists on living in a place the wife doesn't like, she is entitled to a divorce.

MANKOWITZ   This all seems very enlightened, and contrary to the usual picture given of the position of women in Judaism. But I'd like to raise another question. Reverting to the question of the Onah, doesn't it all seem rather calculating and mechanical? Laying down rules for the intimate details of marital life does seem something of an intrusion.

MACCOBY   This is certainly the reaction many Christians, for example, would have. They would regard the laws about frequency of marital intercourse as typical Jewish legalism, as opposed to the free operation of the spirit in Christianity, without need of laws. I would say two things here: first, laws are needed for the protection of the weak. Many wives are neglected sexually, and most systems of law do nothing to protect them from neglect. Also, there is here some measure of protection for men, too. This is relevant today, when many women, in reaction to the oppression of women, are rushing to the opposite extreme, and demanding more of men than is humanly possible, and ignoring the special demands made on a man by his particular profession. Secondly, even marriages which are, on the whole, happy need some guidance—as we see today in the mass of advice offered to married couples by various agencies from Marriage Advice Bureaux to Lonely Hearts columns. These laws of Onah are, in part, advice to couples as to what to expect from each other, and it seems to me wise and

temperate advice. And I think it all to the good
that there is no shyness or prudishness in the
matter; it is frankly discussed, in a way that
Victorians would have found shocking, but which
today we find very refreshing.

Duties of a Wife

This is the work that a wife should do for her husband: grinding flour, baking bread, washing clothes, cooking food, suckling her child, making his bed, and working in wool.

If, however, she brought into the marriage one bondwoman, she need not grind or bake or wash.

If she brought in two bondwomen, she need not cook or suckle her child.

If she brought in three bondwomen, she need not make his bed or work in wool.

If she brought him in four bondwomen, she may sit in a chair all day.

Mishnah, Ketuvot, 5: 5

The Duty of Propagation

Rabbi Eliezer said, 'He who does not engage in the propagation of the human race is like one who sheds blood.'

Rabbi Jacob said, 'It is as if he diminished the Divine Image. For the Torah says, ". . . in the image of God made He man" [Genesis, 9: 6], and then immediately afterwards comes "Be fruitful and multiply".'

Ben Azzai said, 'It is both as if he sheds blood, and as if he diminishes the Divine Image.'

Ben Azzai himself, however, was not married.

They said to Ben Azzai, 'Some preach well and act well, others act well but do not preach well. You come into a different category: you preach well, but do not act well.'

Said Ben Azzai, 'What can I do? My soul is in love with the Torah. Let the world be carried on by others.'

Yevamot, 63b

A NUMERICAL ARGUMENT

Our Rabbis taught: A person who fails to beget a child may cause the Shekhinah [Divine Presence] to depart from Israel.

How can we prove this?

Moses said, 'Return, O Lord, unto the myriads and thousands of Israel' [Numbers, 10: 36].

What is the minimum number denoted by 'myriads and thousands'? Answer: 22,000. [*Note: a 'myriad' means 10,000, and the minimum number denoted by a plural is 2.*] Thus, the Shekhinah does not rest on Israel when they are less than 22,000 in number.

87

Suppose the number of Israel is 21,999. Then any person who has failed to beget a child has caused the Shekhinah to depart from Israel.

Yevamot, 64a

Note. This kind of playful argument is often found in the Aggadah. The principle of 'minimum numbers' is also used in more serious legal arguments.

The Lustfulness of Women

Rabbi Joshua says: A woman prefers lechery with one Kav to chastity with nine Kavs.

Mishnah, Sotah, 3: 4

Note. A Kav is a measure of capacity, roughly equivalent to a pint.

Comment on the above Mishnah by Rabbi Chaim Zundel ben Ephraim Meir: What is meant by 'one Kav' and 'nine Kavs'? The standard commentaries explain 'Kav' as 'a Kav of grain'. The meaning of the Mishnah, then, is that a woman prefers lechery on the poverty-line to chastity in riches, with plentiful supplies of food. Note that 'chastity' includes lawful sexual relations. However, we may arrive at a profounder understanding of the Mishnah by attending to the Gemara in Bava Metsia, 84a: 'Rabbi Johanan said: "The penis of Rabbi Ishmael was like a wine-skin of nine Kavs' capacity." Said Rav Pappa: "The penis of Rabbi Johanan was like a wine-skin of five Kavs' capacity (and some say, of three Kavs' capacity)."* The meaning of the Mishnah, therefore, may be: a woman prefers lechery with a poorly-endowed man to chastity with a well-endowed one.

A CONVERSATION ON THE LUSTFULNESS OF WOMEN

MANKOWITZ   Rabbi Joshua says that a woman prefers sexual pleasure with one Kav to chastity with nine Kavs —a Kav being a measure of capacity roughly

*See p. 26f.

equivalent to a pint. So what he is saying is that a woman prefers lust with one pint to chastity with nine pints.

MACCOBY   This is a rather cryptic saying of which all that one can say with certainty is that it is anti-feminist, and that women are being decried for being over-sexed. This is just the saying of one particular rabbi, who is making the kind of remark that men have always made about women, that women are naturally lecherous. As for the Kavs—the one Kav and the nine Kavs—the usual explanation of this, and perhaps the correct one, is that it refers to quantities of food. A woman prefers a lot of sex with an inadequate supply of food to a lot of food with an inadequate supply of sex.

MANKOWITZ   Does 'sex' refer to marital intercourse or to extramarital intercourse?

MACCOBY   It may refer to promiscuity or adultery, or it may just possibly refer to excessive ordinary marital intercourse—in which case, it is a rather familiar complaint of the inadequate husband about his unsatisfied and insatiable wife: 'Look, I am supplying you with all the necessities of life— you have plenty to eat, but you're still not satisfied, you want more sex.'

MANKOWITZ   It seems a different picture from our society, where books are written to convince people that women have any sexuality at all, and where it is the man who is supposed to be a ravening wolf, out for more sex than he is likely to get.

MACCOBY   Yes, there seems to be little of that kind of *machismo* in the Talmud world. On the contrary, men are regarded as not quite up to the sexual demands of women. In our world, the opposite charge is more likely to be made against women —that they are 'gold-diggers', they prefer nine Kavs of food or money with a rich old sugar-daddy to one Kav with a lusty young im-poverished man.

MANKOWITZ   What I like is your explanation here, in which you bring in the other Talmudic passage about the penis-size of various Rabbis. 'Rabbi Johanan said, "The penis of Rabbi Ishmael was like a wine-skin of nine Kavs. Rabbi Johanan's penis was like a wine-skin of five Kavs' capacity, and some say three Kavs." It was a pretty hefty wine-skin. And you comment that the meaning of our Mishnah here may be that a woman prefers illicit sex with a poorly endowed man to respectable sex with a well endowed one.

MACCOBY   Yes, I don't regard this anti-feminist saying about the lustfulness of women with any great reverence, so I took the liberty of suggesting a somewhat frivolous interpretation of it. Perhaps the Kavs don't refer to food at all, but to penis-size, as in the Talmudic passage which we discussed before. So perhaps what Rabbi Joshua is saying is that a woman prefers a lewd kind of sex with a man who is poorly endowed—has only one Kav capacity—to a more decorous kind of sex with a nine-Kav man. So perhaps what Rabbi Joshua is saying is similar to the kind of comfort given to poorly-endowed men in advice columns and sex manuals—it's not the size that matters.

MANKOWITZ   That is very clear and acceptable, but do you think that, by and large, the Rabbis thought that there was any particular virtue in being well endowed?

MACCOBY   Yes, I think they did. The Rabbis had very great respect for the body. They didn't consider it a virtue to be physically feeble. Just because a man was a student, he didn't have to be emaciated, or be a bowed-down type. This did come into Judaism much later, in the ghettos—the pale, weedy-looking Talmudical student. This is a medieval thing—

MANKOWITZ   And Christian, too.

MACCOBY   Yes, a Christian thing. The idea that the body has to suffer because the spirit is being exercised.

91

The Rabbis of the Talmud didn't have this view. They were aware that hard study makes great physical demands and can have a bad effect on a weak man, and their reaction to this was not to build up a stereotype of a Rabbi as a physical weakling, but on the contrary as a man who needed to be physically very strong in order to cope with the demands of his life. They gloried in telling stories of the physical strength of the Rabbis, and of their physical beauty. Since they regarded sex as an important aspect of life, they even boasted about what huge penises the Rabbis had. Now this, of course, you would never find in the Christian tradition—no one talks about what a huge penis St Jerome had, or St Thomas Aquinas.

MANKOWITZ   Or even Malcolm Muggeridge!

MACCOBY   The Talmud boasts about how much certain Rabbis could eat—they could have won an eating contest! This is the sort of physical gusto that is associated with the Rabbis.

MANKOWITZ   Yet you have admitted that there is an anti-feminist strain in Talmudic thought. Rabbi Joshua seems to disapprove of women, and on the ground that their sexual appetites are too hearty. Perhaps only men are allowed to have hearty appetites?

MACCOBY   Well, of course, there is a puritanical strain in the Talmud, of which Rabbi Joshua's remark is an example. And puritans tend to be anti-feminist too—this is inevitable in any man-dominated society. Still, the opposite tendency exists in the Talmud too. For example, the famous Rabban Johanan ben Zakkai abolished the ordeal for women which we find in the Bible. If a husband suspects his wife of committing adultery, the Bible provides that he can put her through an ordeal, in which she has to drink bitter water, made from the dust of the courtyard of the Temple mixed with water. She has to drink it, and if she is guilty, her belly will distend and she will die in torment. It's a better ordeal, at any rate, than such medieval ones as throwing a witch into water, when it takes a miracle to prove her innocent. Here, it takes a miracle to prove her guilty.

MANKOWITZ Her belly will swell—because of hysterical reasons of guilt.

MACCOBY If the woman felt very guilty, it might happen; if the woman was innocent, or even if she was guilty, it probably didn't happen. The woman had a good chance. Still it was a humiliating ordeal and Rabban Johanan ben Zakkai abolished it, on the very interesting ground that women were not required to undergo such an ordeal unless men as a whole, were above reproach. He proved this, in the usual ingenious way of the Rabbis, from a text, but the thought is both ironic and revolutionary—that men must not expect from women more than they expect from themselves, or seek to use women as a means of drawing attention away from their own inadequacies.

93

The Value of Women

GOD IS A THIEF

The Emperor once said to Rabban Gamaliel, 'Your God is a thief. For he stole one of Adam's ribs.'

The Emperor's daughter was present, and she turned to Rabban Gamaliel and said, 'Leave him to me, and I will answer him.'

She turned to the Emperor and said, 'We must strengthen the guard in this palace. Last night thieves broke in.'

'What did they take?' asked the Emperor.

'They took a silver pitcher. But they left a golden one in its place.'

Said the Emperor, 'I wish such thieves visited us every day!'

Said his daughter, 'That is what Adam said, when he lost a rib and gained a wife.'

Sanhedrin, 39a

Sex

HOW TO HAVE MALE CHILDREN

What should a man do to have male children?

Rabbi Eliezer said: 'He should scatter his money for the poor.'

Rabbi Joshua said: 'He should make his wife happy to take part in the sacred act.'

Bava Batra, 10b

ANOTHER METHOD

Our Rabbis taught: If the woman has her orgasm first, she will bear a male, and if the man has his orgasm first, she will bear a female. Therefore those who restrain themselves in intercourse to enable their wives to have their orgasm first acquire great merit.

Rava said, 'Anyone who wants all his children to be males should have intercourse twice in succession.' [The commentator Rashi explains that by so doing, he is more likely to bring his wife to orgasm.]

Niddah, 31a-b

Note. These remarks show concern for and acceptance of women's enjoyment of intercourse, but for the 'male chauvinist' reason that this will result in the birth of male children, who were more highly prized than female children. It was thought that a woman emits 'seed' during orgasm, and that this 'seed' produces male children, while a man's semen produces female children. Psychologically, this is interesting, for it shows a healthy sense of complementarity between the sexes: the roles of male and female are so complementary that it is the female contribution which produces sons and the male contribution which produces daughters.

DO WHAT YOU LIKE

Rabbi Johanan ben Dahabai said: Four things were told to me by the Ministering Angels: why do people become lame? because they 'turn their table' (have intercourse from the rear); why do people become blind? because they gaze at 'that place' (the female genitals); why do they become dumb? because they kiss 'that place'; why do they become deaf? because they talk while having intercourse.

Said Rabbi Johanan: These are the words of Rabbi Johanan ben Dahabai, but the Sages say, 'The Halakhah is not according to Johanan ben Dahabai; but anything that a man wants to do with his wife he may do. It is just like meat that comes from the butcher's; if he wants to eat it with salt, he may do so, if he wants to eat it roasted, or boiled, or seethed, he may do so; and the same applies to fish.'

Nedarim, 20b

Note. This passage reflects both the puritanical and the anti-puritanical strain in the Talmud. The majority opinion is anti-puritanical; yet in the Middle Ages, the puritans won the day, probably because of the gloom of exile. It is interesting that the Sages refuse to be brow-beaten by Rabbi Johanan ben Dabahai's claim to the authority of the Ministering Angels; or even by his terrifying threats of punishment for sexual variations. (According to another possible translation, the threats were not to the couple having intercourse but to the resulting offspring, an even more unattractive idea.)

THE WILLING WIFE

Rabbi Samuel ben Nahmani said in the name of Rabbi Johanan: a man whose wife asks him for intercourse will have sons greater than the generation of the wilderness.

But is not a 'brazen' wife elsewhere condemned?

What is meant is not that she openly asks him for intercourse, but indirectly shows that she wants it, and disposes his mind towards it.

Nedarim, 20b

LEARNING ABOUT SEX

Rav Kahana once went in and hid under Rav's bed to see how his teacher conducted himself in intercourse with his wife. He noted that Rav chatted and joked with his wife before having intercourse with her.

Said Rav Kahana, 'It is as if the mouth of Father had never tasted such food before!'

Said Rav, 'Kahana, are you here? Go out, for it is not good manners.'

Said he to him, 'It is Torah, and I have to learn.'

Note. See also page 151.

Husband and Wife

Rav was constantly tormented by his wife. If he asked her to cook lentils for him, she would cook peas. If he asked for peas, she would cook lentils.

His son Hiyya used to carry the messages between his father and mother. At first, he transmitted the messages exactly as his father told him, but as he became older and wiser, he noticed that his mother always did the opposite, so he changed the messages. When his father asked for lentils, Hiyya told his mother peas, and vice versa. As a result, Rav always got what he wanted to eat.

One day, Rav said to his son, 'Your mother has improved.'

Said Hiyya, 'That is because I reversed your messages.'

Said Rav, 'It is well said by the people, "Thine own offspring teaches thee reason." Nevertheless, do not so any more, for Scripture is a higher authority than the people, and Scripture says, "They have taught their tongue to speak lies" [Jeremiah, 9: 4].'

Yevamot, 63a

THE CONTRADICTION

Rav Judah was studying the Bible with his son Rav Isaac. They came to the verse, 'I find a woman more bitter than death' [Ecclesiastes, 7: 26].

Said Rav Isaac, 'What kind of woman is meant here?'

Said Rav Judah, 'Someone like your mother.'

On another occasion Rav Judah taught his son as follows: 'A man finds happiness only with his first wife, as the Bible says, "Let thy fountain be blessed, and have joy of the wife of thy youth" [Proverbs, 5: 18].'

Said Rav Isaac, 'What kind of woman is meant here?'

Said Rav Judah, 'Someone like your mother.'

Is there not a contradiction between these two teachings of Rav Judah?

No, for though his wife was very bad-tempered, she could easily be appeased by a kindly word.

Yevamot, 63a

Divorce

GROUNDS FOR DIVORCE

These are compelled to give their wives a divorce, if the wife so desires:
>   one who is afflicted with boils;
>   one who has polypus, which causes bad breath;
>   one who collects dog's excrement for a living;
>   a coppersmith;
>   a tanner.

Even if the wife knew about it before they were married, the husband must divorce her if she requests it.

Rabbi Meir said: Even if the husband made it a condition with her to marry him in spite of one of these defects, she may say, 'I thought that I could endure it, but now I see that I cannot.'

But the Sages say: If it was a condition of the marriage, she must endure it.

Mishnah, Ketuvot, 7: 10

AGAINST DIVORCE

Said Rabbi Eleazar, 'If a man divorces his first wife, even the Altar sheds tears.'

Said Rabbi Johanan, 'He that puts his wife away is hated of God.'

Gittin, 90b

Note. These expressions may seem to be at variance with the fact that divorce is easy in Jewish law. In practice, the fact that

Jewish couples are not bound together irrevocably for life and are at liberty to resort to divorce if the marriage goes wrong has given an atmosphere of free affection to Jewish marriages, and the loyalty of Jewish husbands and wives has become proverbial. The above expressions show also that Jewish 'legalism' is always tempered by extra-legal considerations; what is legally allowed is not always approved, and the fixing of a law may be only the beginning (but an essential beginning) of the moulding of a moral attitude. The rigid Christian law forbidding divorce shows too great reliance on law, strangely enough, as a moral factor.

Contraception

During the twenty-four months after the birth of a baby, a husband may 'thresh within and winnow without' (i.e. practise *coitus interruptus*, so that the suckling of the child should not be cut short by a further pregnancy). These are the words of Rabbi Eliezer.

They said to him, 'Surely this was the sin of Er and Onan [see Genesis, 38: 9 . . . 'when he went in unto his brother's wife he spilt it on the ground].'

No, it is not the same, for they not only 'threshed within and winnowed without', but also practised anal intercourse.

Yevamot, 34b

Note. The commentary Tosaphot raises the difficulty that anal intercourse is not forbidden either. Yet the liberal attitude of Rabbi Eliezer was overborne in the Middle Ages by anxieties about the sinfulness of 'wasting seed'.

Honouring One's Mother

Rabbi Tarfon used to show honour for his mother by bending down to let her step on him when she ascended or descended from her bed. One day, he boasted to his colleagues in the academy about this. They said to him, 'You have not yet reached half the honour due to a mother.'

Rabbi Joseph, when he heard his mother approaching, used to say, 'Let me rise up before the approaching Presence of God.'

Kiddushin, 31b

Inheritance of Daughters

If someone died and left both sons and daughters: if he left a large estate, the sons inherit it, and the daughters are maintained out of it. But if he left a small estate, the daughters are maintained out of it, and the sons receive nothing [literally: 'go begging round the houses'].

Mishnah, Ketuvot, 13: 3 (also Bava Batra, 9: 1

Note. See also page 138.

Beruriah

Beruriah (a name probably derived from the Roman name Valeria), was famous for her learning, and is regarded as a Talmudic authority. She was the daughter of the martyr Rabbi Hananiah ben Teradion, and the wife of the even more famous Rabbi Meir.

Rabbi Simlai came before Rabbi Johanan and asked him to teach him the Book of Genealogies [a commentary on the Book of Chronicles]. At first Rabbi Johanan refused, but later agreed.

Said Rabbi Simlai, 'I intend to devote three months to this study.'

Upon this, Rabbi Johanan threw a clod of earth at him in disgust, saying, 'Even Beruriah, the wife of Rabbi Meir and the daughter of Rabbi Hananiah ben Teradion took more than three years over this study, and you propose to do it in three months! And she once studied 300 topics from 300 teachers in one day!'

Pesachim, 62b

HER SHARPNESS OF TONGUE

Rabbi Jose the Galilean was once on a journey when he met Beruriah.

He asked her, 'By what road shall we go to Lydda?'

Said she, 'Foolish Galilean, have not the Sages said, "Do not waste words when talking to a woman?" You should have said, "How to Lydda?" '

Eruvin, 53b

Note. This rather puzzling anecdote seems to show Beruriah as arrogant and humble at the same time—arrogant in her forthright rebuke to the famous Rabbi Jose the Galilean, and humble in her acceptance of an anti-feminist rabbinical saying. Perhaps she took the remark in a pro-feminist way: 'Be especially careful to display wisdom and respect when talking to a woman by avoiding boring, condescending garrulousness.' The expression 'foolish Galilean' is evidence of the humorous rivalry between Judeans and Galileans (cf. Dr Johnson's remarks about Scotsmen).

A MEDIEVAL LEGEND

There is a legend about Beruriah, found in a medieval source (Rashi, Avodah Zarah, 18b) but not in the Talmud.

Once Beruriah scoffed at the rabbinical saying, 'Women are light-minded' [Kiddushin, 80b]. Rabbi Meir, her husband said, 'By your life, in the end you will agree with this.' He told one of his students to tempt her to adultery. After urging her for many days, he persuaded her to agree. When she found out what had happened, she hanged herself; and Rabbi Meir went away to Babylonia because of the disgrace.

Note. This story is wrongly attributed to the Talmud in a Note in the Soncino translation of the Talmud (Av. Zar. 18b). The story appears to be a medieval anti-feminist concoction, and is very different in spirit from the Talmudic references to Beruriah. The story was invented in order to account for the Talmud's cryptic remark that Rabbi Meir went away to Babylonia 'because of the matter of Beruriah'. The true explanation of this remark is probably that Rabbi Meir had to flee to Babylonia because of trouble with the Roman authorities arising from his efforts to free Beruriah's sister from slavery in Rome.

By the way, Rashi's story is often wrongly quoted to mean that Beruriah actually did commit adultery with Rabbi Meir's student. The story does not say this; but that she consented to do so, and was then told the truth about Rabbi Meir's plan to test her and prove the soundness of the rabbinical remark about the light-mindedness of women. The story is unpleasant enough without adding to its unpleasantness.

106

THE RUNNING ARGUMENT

The Value of Argument

Said Rabbi Hiyya bar Abba: 'Even a father and a son, or a master and his pupil, become enemies of each other when they study the same topic; yet they do not stir from there until they come to love each other—as it is written, "The wars of the Lord end in love" [Numbers, 21: 14].'

Kiddushin, 30b

Note. It is only by some playful punning on place names that Rabbi Hiyya extracts this meaning from the Hebrew of Numbers, 21: 14, which says literally: 'Wherefore it is written in the book of the wars of the Lord, "Vaheb in Suphah . . ."' (Vaheb and Suphah are place names but 'Vaheb' is a pun for 'love' and 'Suphah' is a pun for 'end'.)

RABBI JOHANAN AND RESH LAKISH

Resh Lakish was a bandit, famous for his strength and daring.

One day, Rabbi Johanan was bathing in the River Jordan. Resh Lakish saw him and leapt into the Jordan after him.

Rabbi Johanan said to him, 'Strength like yours should be for the Torah.'

Resh Lakish said, 'Beauty like yours should be for women.'

Said Rabbi Johanan, 'If you will repent, I will give you my sister in marriage. She is even more beautiful than I am.'

Resh Lakish agreed to this; and found immediately that some of his strength had departed.

Rabbi Johanan taught him Bible and Mishnah, and he became an accepted scholar.

One day, there was a dispute in the academy on the question,

'What constitutes the final stage of the manufacture of a sword, a knife, a dagger, a spear, a hand-saw and a scythe?' Rabbi Johanan answered, 'When they are hardened in the furnace.' Resh Lakish said, 'No, it is when they are steeled in water.' Rabbi Johanan said, 'A robber understands his trade.'

Resh Lakish, annoyed, said, 'And what good has it done me to cease to be a robber? I was a leader there, and was called "Master", and here too I am called "Master".'

Said Rabbi Johanan, 'What good has it done you? You have been brought under the wings of the Divine Presence.'

As a result of the displeasure felt by Rabbi Johanan, Resh Lakish became ill. After a while, he died.

Rabbi Johanan grieved very much for him. Said the Rabbis, 'Who shall go to take his mind away from his grief? Let Rabbi Eleazar ben Pedath go, for he has a very subtle mind.'

Rabbi Eleazar went and sat before Rabbi Johanan. Every time Rabbi Johanan uttered an opinion, he said, 'There is a Baraitha* which supports your opinion.'

Said Rabbi Johanan, 'You are not like the son of Lakish. Whenever I stated an opinion, the son of Lakish used to make twenty-four objections, to which I was compelled to give twenty-four answers; and so the understanding of the Law was broadened. You, however, say, "There is a Baraitha which supports you." Do I not know myself that my opinions are correct?'

He continued to tear his garments and weep, saying, 'Where are you, son of Lakish?' Eventually, he lost his reason; so the Rabbis prayed for him, and he died.

Bava Metsia, 84a

---

*'Baraitha' means an 'external source', i.e. a passage from some compilation other than the Mishnah, the main authority for Rabbinic law. Everybody knew the Mishnah, but special learning or tradition was sometimes needed to quote a Baraitha.

Accepting Majority Decisions

After the destruction of the Temple in 70 CE, the surviving Sages met at Yavneh to collate the Law, and reduce it to writing. Since the Oral Law, in Temple times, had been handed on by word of mouth, and the troubles of the Roman Occupation had disrupted the process of tradition, many laws were disputed. Various Rabbis now came forward and 'testified' about the laws that they had received by oral tradition, but these 'testimonies' sometimes conflicted, and some of them had to be rejected, by the process of majority vote. These 'testimonies' are preserved in the earliest Tractate of the Mishnah, called Eduyot *('Testimonies'). As we see from the following story, much heart-searching was caused to individual Rabbis whose 'testimonies' were rejected.*

THE TESTIMONIES OF AKAVYA

Akavya ben Mahalaleel gave 'testimony' of four matters of the Law, but his evidence was overruled by his colleagues on all four matters. Akavya, however, continued to hold that the Law was according to his evidence, and he refused to accept the decision of his colleagues.

They said to him, 'Akavya, if you will change your mind about the four matters, we will make you Vice-President of the High Court of Israel.'

Said Akavya, 'It is better that I should be called an idiot all my days, than that I should become a sinner for one hour before the All-present; and so I should be, if I changed my mind for the sake of office.'

As he continued obdurate, his colleagues excommunicated

him, and he died while still under sentence of excommunication, so they put a stone on his coffin.*

While he was on his death-bed, he said to his son, 'My son, retract the four opinions which I gave.'

Said his son, 'If so, why did not you yourself retract?'

Said Akavya, 'I heard those opinions as majority decisions of an assembly of Rabbis, and those Rabbis heard them as majority decisions of other assemblies of Rabbis, and that is why I have stood by my opinion, just as they stood by theirs. But you, my son, have heard these opinions only as the opinions of an individual, myself, and you have heard contrary opinions from the majority of an assembly of Rabbis. It is better to forsake the opinion of an individual and cleave to the opinion of a majority.'

Eduyot, 5: 6

THE HOUSE OF HILLEL AND THE HOUSE OF SHAMMAI

At an early period, the Rabbis divided into two schools, called the House of Hillel and the House of Shammai, following the rulings of the famous teachers Hillel and Shammai respectively. The Houses never became separate sects, and, though they argued fiercely, they came to an accommodation.

Said Rav Abba in the name of Samuel:† 'For three years there was a dispute between the House of Shammai and the House of Hillel, both saying, "The Law is in accordance with our views."

Finally, a heavenly voice went forth, saying, "Both the words of the House of Hillel and the words of the House of Shammai are the words of the Living God, but the *halakhah* [law] is in accordance with the House of Hillel." '

But since both were the words of the Living God, by what right did the House of Hillel become the authority for *halakhah*?

*This was the custom when someone died while under sentence of excommunication. The stone symbolized the punishment of 'stoning'.

†I.e. Rav Abba reported a tradition which he received from his teacher, Samuel. Statements in the Talmud are often introduced in this way, as it was considered meritorious to 'report a saying in the name of him who said it'.

112

They were the more humble and the more inclined to yield, and paid as much attention to the opinions of the House of Shammai as to their own opinions.

Eruvin, 13b

FIXING THE CALENDAR

The Jewish calendar was a lunar calendar, in which a month might be either 29 or 30 days, depending on when the new moon was observed to appear. Only when two witnesses had appeared before the Court in Jerusalem (later at Yavneh) to give evidence that they had seen the new moon with their own eyes, could the start of a new month be proclaimed. There was some difference of opinion among the Rabbis about how such evidence should be assessed: should it be very critically examined and rejected if it contained contradictions, or should the witnesses be given the benefit of the doubt? This question could affect the whole calendar, and in particular the dates assigned to the great Festivals and Fasts, such as the Day of Atonement. The following story shows how a great Rabbi, who thought that the Day of Atonement had been fixed for the wrong day, nevertheless humbled himself to accept the decision duly fixed by process of law.

Rabban Gamaliel, President of the Court in Yavneh had pictures of various shapes of the moon [in various phases] on tablets on the wall of his room. When witnesses came to give evidence of having seen the new moon, he would show them the diagrams and say, 'Did you see it this shape, or that shape?'

One day, two witnesses came, and said, 'We saw the moon in the east in the morning, and in the west in the evening of the same day.' When Rabbi Johanan ben Nuri heard this, he said, 'They are false witnesses.' But when they came to Yavneh, Rabban Gamaliel accepted their evidence. [He accepted that they had seen the moon in the west in the evening, and thought that they must have seen an optical illusion in the morning, and were not deliberately lying.]

Another time, two witnesses came and said, 'We saw the new moon at the expected time, but on the next day it did not appear.' And Rabban Gamaliel accepted their evidence of having seen the new moon.

Said Rabbi Dosa ben Hyrcanus, 'They are false witnesses. How can one testify of a woman that she has given birth to a child, when the next day her belly is between her teeth [i.e. she is obviously still pregnant]?'

Said Rabbi Joshua to him, 'I agree with you.' Rabbi Joshua therefore refused to accept the ruling of Rabban Gamaliel and his Court fixing the new month according to the evidence of these witnesses. And, as it happened, the month in question was the month of Tishri, which contains the Day of Atonement.

Rabban Gamaliel sent to Rabbi Joshua, saying, 'I decree that you should come to me carrying your staff and your money-purse on the Day of Atonement which is according to your reckoning.' [To carry a staff or money on the Day of Atonement is strictly forbidden. Rabban Gamaliel required a practical demonstration by Rabbi Joshua that he had relinquished his own ruling and accepted that of Rabban Gamaliel and his Court.]

Rabbi Akiva went to visit Rabbi Joshua and found him in distress. Said Rabbi Akiva, 'You must accept Rabban Gamaliel's ruling even if you think it is wrong. For God Himself accepts the rulings of duly appointed representatives of Israel, even when they are wrong. How can this be proved from Scripture? "These are the set feasts of the Lord . . . which you shall proclaim" [Leviticus, 23: 4]. It is for you to proclaim them, says God; whether they are at the right time or the wrong time, I have no other set feasts except the ones which you, through your representatives, proclaim.'

Rabbi Joshua was still not quite convinced, so he went to visit Rabbi Dosa ben Hyrcanus, who urged the same considerations as Rabbi Akiva. Said Rabbi Dosa ben Hyrcanus, 'If we criticise the court of Rabban Gamaliel, we shall have to criticise every court which has arisen from the days of Moses until now.'

On the day that was the Day of Atonement according to his own reckoning, Rabbi Joshua took his staff and his money-purse in his hand, and went to Yavneh to Rabban Gamaliel.

Then Rabban Gamaliel stood up and kissed Rabbi Joshua on the head, and said to him, 'Greetings to you, my master, and my disciple. You are my master in wisdom, but you are my disciple in that you have accepted my words.'

Rosh Hashanah, 2: 8-9

Arguing for Pleasure

THE KOY

If one man saw a *koy* [an animal that was believed to be inter-
mediate between a kid and a gazelle, and which, consequently,
the Rabbis were uncertain to classify as wild or domestic, or
both or neither], and said, 'I vow to be a Nazarite if this is a
wild animal', and another man said, 'I vow to be a Nazarite if
this is not a wild animal', and a third man said, 'I vow to be a
Nazarite if this is a domestic animal', and a fourth man said, 'I
vow to be a Nazarite if this is not a domestic animal', and a
fifth man said, 'I vow to be a Nazarite if this is both a wild
animal and a domestic animal', and a sixth man said, 'I vow
to be a Nazarite if this is neither a wild animal nor a domestic
animal', and a seventh man said, 'I vow to be a Nazarite if one
of you six people is a Nazarite', and an eighth man said, 'I
vow to be a Nazarite if none of you seven people is a Nazarite',
and a ninth man said, 'I vow to be a Nazarite if all you eight
people are Nazarites'—then they are all Nazarites.

Mishnah, Nazir, 5: 7

*Note. For the details of the Nazarite vow, see Numbers, 6: 1-21.
A Nazarite had to refrain from cutting his hair, from ritual
uncleanliness deriving from touching a corpse, from drinking
wine, and from eating anything that comes from a vine. The
most famous Nazarite was Samson, whose vow was life-long,
but most Nazarites vowed for a period of thirty days.*

*A man who vowed to be a Nazarite in a 'doubtful' way had to
fulfil the vow, and the Mishnah uses the example of the* koy *to
illustrate how doubt could arise in a hypothetical form of vow.*

116

The logical and legal problems arising from the koy *fascinated the Rabbis, and are found in other contexts, e.g. the laws of slaughtering animals, and of uncleanliness.*

THE MOUSE AND THE PIECE OF BREAD

On the eve of Passover, the house should be searched to make sure that no leavened bread remains on the premises.

Rava asked a question: 'Suppose a mouse entered a room, which had already been searched, with a piece of bread in its mouth, and a mouse then came out of the room with a piece of bread in its mouth. Can one assume that the mouse (and bread) that came out are the same mouse and bread that went in? [In which case no further search is necessary.] Or is it perhaps a different mouse?'

Rava then went on to ask: 'Suppose that the answer to my first question is that there is no need to assume a different mouse; what if a white mouse went in with bread in its mouth and a black mouse came out with bread in its mouth? Must one assume that it is a different piece of bread or can one suppose that it is the same piece of bread which the first mouse threw away and the second mouse picked up?

Perhaps you will say, "Mice do not take food from each other." In that case, what if a mouse went in with a piece of bread in its mouth and a weasel came out with a piece of bread in its mouth? Can one assume that the weasel took away the bread from the mouse, or could it be another piece of bread, since a weasel would have the mouse itself in its mouth? Suppose then that the weasel had the mouse *and* the bread in its mouth? But surely (if it were the same piece of bread) the weasel would have the mouse in its mouth and the bread would still be in the mouse's mouth? But perhaps the mouse dropped the bread in its fear and the weasel picked up the mouse and the bread separately?'

The problem was left unsolved.

Pesachim, 10b

It is forbidden to shave with a razor the 'corners of the beard' [see Leviticus, 19:27]. This is one of the two negative commandments which do not apply to women (Mishnah).

How do we know that this commandment does not apply to women?

There are two ways of proving this. One is by reasoning, and the other is by exegesis.

The proof by reasoning is that women do not have beards, (or if they do, it does not count as a beard within the meaning of the act).

The proof by exegesis is as follows. The Torah says, 'You shall not round the corner of your heads, nor shalt thou mar the corner of thy beard.' Why does the Torah switch from the plural ['you shall not'] to the singular ['thou shalt not'] in the course of this sentence? The effect is to give special emphasis to the singular 'thou' and 'thy': '*thou* shalt not mar the corner of *thy* beard'; i.e. the law applies only to *thy* beard, not to thy wife's beard.

Kiddushin, 35b

THE COMMANDMENT NOT TO BE POOR

Ilfa and Rabbi Johanan studied the Torah together. However, they found themselves in great want, so they said to each other, 'Let us go and engage in commerce, so that we may fulfil the commandment, "There shall be no poor man among you" [Deuteronomy, 15:4].'

They journeyed away, and came to a wall, where they sat down. The wall was in fact in a precarious state. While they were having their meal, two angels came, and Rabbi Johanan heard them talking to one another.

'Let us throw down this wall,' said one, 'and kill these two people, because they are forsaking the life of the World to Come, and busying themselves with the life of an hour.'

'No,' said the other. 'Leave them alone. One of them is destined for a great hour.'

Rabbi Johanan said to Ilfa, 'Master, did you hear anything?'

'No,' said Ilfa.

Said Rabbi Johanan to himself, 'Since I heard this, and Ilfa did not, I must be the one who is destined for a great hour.' He then spoke aloud to Ilfa: 'I will go back.'

Said Ilfa, 'And what about fulfilling the commandment, "There shall be no poor man among you"?'

Said Rabbi Johanan, 'Instead, I will fulfil the commandment, "The poor shall never cease out of the land" [Deuteronomy, 15: 11].'

Ta'anit, 21a

Note. Of course, the two verses cited were not really commandments, but predictions. It suited the humour of the two young scholars, however, to treat them as commandments.

The difficulty of the contradiction between the two texts is answered elsewhere in the Talmud: 'If you deserve it, there will be no poor man among you, but if not, the poor will never cease out of the land.'

Arguing in Earnest

BETTER NOT TO BE BORN?

For two and a half years the House of Shammai and the House of Hillel disputed. The House of Shammai argued that it would have been better for man not to have been created; and the House of Hillel argued that it was better for man to have been created than not to have been created.

In the end, a vote was taken, and it was decided: 'It would have been better for man not to have been created, but now that he has been created, let him scrutinize his deeds.'

Eruvin, 13b

THE PRIEST'S DAUGHTER

According to the Bible (Leviticus, 21: 9), the daughter of a priest who 'plays the harlot' has to be executed by burning. This is one of many Biblical laws which the Rabbis of the Talmud, following the Pharisees, refused to accept at their face-value. They could not expunge such laws from Holy Writ, but they hedged them round with so many restrictions and qualifications that, in effect, they became null and void. By ingenious interpretations of Biblical expressions, the Rabbis deduced that the execution of the priest's daughter did not apply to an unmarried daughter; nor did it apply to a married daughter; it applied only to a betrothed daughter, before her marriage; and it did not apply to any betrothed daughter, but only to one between the ages of 12 and 12½. This very narrow definition (together with the strict laws of evidence which hedged round and made unlikely any sentence of capital punishment) ensured that the burning of a priest's daughter would never actually take place.

120

Rabbi Akiva, however, took a less lenient view about the priest's daughter, not because he was more severe generally in penal matters (he once declared that he would never regard evidence as adequate for capital punishment), but for exegetical reasons connected with his own special methods of interpreting texts. Rabbi Ishmael, representing the majority view of the Rabbis, takes Rabbi Akiva to task, in the following dialogue, for putting considerations of exegesis before considerations of humanity.

When Scripture speaks of 'the daughter of a priest who plays the harlot', this refers only to a girl between the ages of 12 and 12½ who is betrothed but not yet married. These are the words of Rabbi Ishmael.

Rabbi Akiva said, 'A priest's daughter is punished by fire whether she is betrothed or married.'

Said Rabbi Ishmael to Rabbi Akiva, 'You know that the text Deuteronomy, 22: 23 throws light on this matter. Just as that text proves that an unmarried girl is excluded from this penalty, so the same text proves that all girls are excluded who are not betrothed and between the ages of 12 and 12½.'

Said Rabbi Akiva, 'My brother, I would agree with you entirely, were it not that our present text contains the superfluous word, "and", and in accordance with my method of exegesis, by which I give a legal interpretation to all the superfluous "ands" in the Torah, I here interpret that the superfluous "and" means that a married girl is also subject to the penalty.'

Said Rabbi Ishmael, 'Are we going to burn a woman to death because you interpret an additional "and"?'

Sanhedrin, 51b

THE THIRTEEN METHODS OF EXEGESIS

(Translation from S. Singer's Prayer Book, with a few alterations.)

Rabbi Ishmael says: 'There are thirteen methods by which the Torah may be interpreted, so that its implications are drawn out.
Method 1. The *a fortiori* argument.
Method 2. Inference from similarity of expressions used in separate verses.

Method 3. A general law may be derived by induction from different cases which, occurring in the same or in different verses, have yet some feature in common.

Method 4. A general proposition followed by the enumeration of particulars already comprehended in the general proposition (in which case the scope of the proposition is limited by the things specified). [*Note. The Hebrew of which the foregoing is the translation consists of two words.*]

Method 5. An enumeration of particulars followed by a general proposition in which they are comprehended (in which case the scope of the proposition extends also to the things not specified). [*Note. Two words of Hebrew again.*]

Method 6. Two general propositions, separated from each other by an enumeration of particulars, include only such things as are similar to those specified.

Method 7. An inference drawn from a general proposition complemented by a particular term, and an inference drawn from a particular term complemented by a general proposition.

Method 8. If anything is included in a general proposition and is then made the subject of a special statement, that which is predicated of it is not to be understood as limited to itself alone, but is to be applied to the whole of the general proposition.

Method 9. If anything is included in a general proposition, and is then singled out in order to be made the subject of a special statement, similar to the general proposition, this particularization is intended, so far as its subject is concerned, to lessen and not to add to its restrictions.

Method 10. If anything is included in a general proposition, and is then singled out in order to be made the subject of a special statement, not similar to the general proposition, this particularization is intended in some respects to lessen and in others to add to its restrictions.

Method 11. If anything is included in a general proposition, and is then made the subject of a fresh statement (not in harmony with the former), the terms of the general proposition will not apply to it, unless the Scripture distinctly indicates that they shall apply.

Method 12. The meaning of a passage may be deduced from its context, or from some subsequent passage.

Method 13. Similarly, when two passages arc in contradiction to each other, the explanation can be determined only when a third text is found that can harmonize the two.

Note. The above methods are constantly used in the Talmud in order to draw out the logical implications of Biblical texts. Some of the methods are literary-critical, but most are in the category of inductive logic, and show interesting similarities to the inductive principles enunciated by philosophers of science such as John Stuart Mill. The basic principle is that the Torah is an entirely logical text, which is unlikely; yet it is logical enough to come out of this process of fine sifting with considerable credit.

A DISCUSSION ABOUT SQUATTING

Rabbi Hisda said to Rami bar Hama, 'You were not with us yesterday in the House of Study where some very interesting topics were discussed.'

Said Rami bar Hama, 'What were these very interesting topics?'

Said Rav Hisda, 'We discussed this subject: suppose someone went and lived for a while in a courtyard belonging to someone else without the latter's knowledge, should he afterwards pay him rent? The discussion took the following lines: what are the circumstances envisaged by the question? It cannot be that the courtyard could not have been hired out to someone else and that the squatter could have had free lodging elsewhere, for what liability could there be where the defendant derived no benefit and the plaintiff sustained no loss? On the other hand, it cannot be the direct opposite—that the courtyard could have been hired to someone else and the squatter could not have had free lodging elsewhere—for in these circumstances why should there *not* be a liability, since the defendant derived a benefit and the plaintiff incurred a loss? The problem must arise in the case where the premises were not for hire and the squatter could not have had free lodging elsewhere. Is the squatter entitled to plead, "What loss have I caused you?" Or can the owner say, "You have derived a benefit and so must pay rent" ?'

Rama bar Hama then said, 'The solution to the problem is contained in a Mishnah.'

'What Mishnah?'

'Before I tell you that,' said Rami bar Hama, 'you will have to perform some service for me.'

So Rav Hisda took his scarf and folded it for him.

Then Rami bar Hama said to him, 'The Mishnah is this one: "If an animal did damage with its teeth to objects lying on public ground, the owner of the animal is not liable to pay compensation to the owner of the objects. If, however, the animal derived benefit from the damage done by it, the owner of the animal must repay the extent of the benefit." '

Rav Hisda accepted this solution, since the Mishnah seems to show that benefit derived must be paid for.

When the conversation was reported to Rava, he commented, 'How lucky a person is who has God on his side! Rami bar Hama escaped the following refutation: the case in the Mishnah is quite different from the case of the squatter. In the case in the Mishnah the defendant derived a benefit and the plaintiff sustained a loss, whereas in the case of the squatter the defendant derived a benefit but the plaintiff sustained no loss.'

But Rami bar Hama's view cannot be so easily refuted, for, in his opinion, goods left on public ground have been abandoned by their owner and the animal therefore cannot be regarded as the exclusive cause of the loss.

Bava Kamma, 20a

Note. The question is discussed further at some length, various precedents being adduced and refuted as differing in some respect from the case under discussion. The final opinion is that no rent need be paid by the squatter, since he actually confers a benefit on the owner by preventing dilapidation of the premises which would occur if they remained unoccupied.

A RABBINICAL ARGUMENT

If a man A dies childless, his brother B is required to marry

124

the widow C (though he may instead 'divorce' her by the ceremony known as Halitzah).

However, a rabbinical law requires that the consummation of this marriage should be postponed for three months, so that a child born 7–9 months after the death of the previous husband should be clearly known to have been fathered by that husband, not by the new husband.

Suppose, however, that B consummates the marriage immediately, in contravention of the rabbinical law, and a child is born to C seven months later. There is thus some doubt whether the child is a 7-month child fathered by B or a 9-month child fathered by A.

The Talmudic law is now as follows: the child thus born is fully legitimate, but the *next* child born in the marriage is a 'doubtful bastard'!

The reason behind this apparently illogical law is that a marriage between B and C (widow and brother-in-law) is actually *forbidden* (Leviticus, 18: 16), the *sole* exception being the case before us, when the first marriage was childless, when the marriage becomes obligatory instead.

Consequently, the doubt whether the first child was fathered by A or B is also a doubt whether the marriage between B and C was legitimate. When a second child is born, therefore (the father this time being definitely B), there is doubt whether the child is legitimate or not and the child has the status of 'doubtful bastard'.

The first child is fully legitimate, however, on any reckoning. If he is fathered by the first husband A, he was conceived in legitimate wedlock. If he was fathered by the second husband B, then the first marriage was childless, and the second marriage is therefore legitimate, making the child legitimately born.

The law, therefore, is entirely logical.

A POINT OF LOGIC

If an ox does damage by goring with its horn, its owner has to pay *half* the cost only [see Exodus, 21: 35], unless the ox has proved itself a habitual gorer (in which case the owner must pay the full cost).

If, however, an ox does damage with its teeth or feet (in normal circumstances), the full cost must be paid even on the first occasion of damage (the owner being required to guard against such foreseeable damage). This applies, however, only when the damage takes place on the premises of the plaintiff, not in a public place, where the owner of the ox cannot be held responsible for goods left lying around by the plaintiff. On the other hand, the half-damages incurred through *goring* ('Horn') have to be paid even if the goring happened in a public place.

Question: If an ox does damage by Horn on the premises of the plaintiff, does the defendant have to pay half-damages or full damages?

Rabbi Tarfon says: 'Full damages.' The Sages say: 'Half-damages.'

Rabbi Tarfon's opinion is based on an *a fortiori* argument, as follows: If Tooth and Foot, which are not penalized at all in a public place, are nevertheless the occasion of Full Damages on the plaintiff's premises, surely Horn which *is* to some extent penalized in a public place must occasion Full Damages on the plaintiff's premises.

To this the Sages reply: We cannot accept Rabbi Tarfon's argument, as it infringes a principle of the logic of the *a fortiori* argument, namely that the conclusion of such an argument cannot *add* to the terms contained in its data. It is permissible to argue that since Horn is penalized by Half-damages in a public place, it should be penalized *a fortiori* by Half-damages in the plaintiff's premises, but not that the damages should be increased from half to full.

Bava Kamma, 25a (Mishnah, 2: 5)

ESSAY: THE OX THAT GORED

The Talmud always assumes that the Torah is very intelligently written, since its author is God, the most intelligent of all beings.

Thus, the Torah distinguishes between different kinds of damage done to property by an ox: by goring, by trampling, and by eating (the Talmud calls these, for short, Horn, Foot and Tooth). These distinctions are not arbitrary—they correspond to real differences in the legal circumstances of the damage.

Damage by *Horn* shows aggressive behaviour by the animal. Such behaviour is somewhat unusual, and therefore the responsibility of the owner of the animal is less. Suppose, for example, an ox were to cause damage to goods by attempting to perform a juggling-act with them—no owner could be expected to foresee such behaviour on the part of his ox. Goring with the horns is not as unexpected as that, but it is somewhat unusual, and, therefore, damage caused in this way does not incur a full penalty. The owner has to pay only half the value of the damage caused.

If, however, this is not the first time the ox has done damage with its horns, the behaviour is not so unexpected. On the *third* occasion of goring, full damages must be paid, as the owner is expected to have noted by now the fact that his animal has this unusual pattern of behaviour and to take appropriate precautions.

Note that although this kind of damage is called 'Horn', it is not the actual literal use of the horns that is meant. Any kind of aggressive damage whether with the feet, or the teeth, or any other part of the animal's anatomy comes under the heading 'Horn'. It is typical of the Talmud to give a concrete name such as 'Horn' to some life-situation, and then to refine the definition of it in such a way that the concrete label covers an abstractly-defined syndrome of situation-traits. The concrete label 'Horn' is a device which aids the imagination more than abstract legalese such as 'more than usually aggressive behaviour by an animal resulting in damage to property', and the use of the horns is in fact the most frequently encountered form of such aggressive behaviour. The Talmud thus combines, in its own special manner, imaginative realism with abstract precision of thought.

'Tooth' and 'Foot' (eating and trampling) have their own special characteristics by which they differ from each other, but we may ignore this aspect for the present and merely note that both of them, in contrast to Horn, are *usual* modes of damage, i.e. any normal animal may be expected to eat whatever it comes across that is eatable, or to tread on anything that happens to lie in its path. If, on the other hand, an animal eats something *unusual*, for example, table-cloths, or goes out of its way to tread on something, this would count as aggressive or unusual behaviour, i.e. Horn.

The question now arises of *where* the damage takes place. Suppose I deposit my china tea-set in my neighbour's field, and his ox tramples on it? Does the ox's owner have to pay for the damage? No, because I had no business to place my belongings in someone else's field.

But suppose I happen to place my china tea-set in my *own* field, and my neighbour's ox strays into my field and tramples on my china tea-set? The ox's owner must pay for the damage, since it is his responsibility to see that his ox does not stray. Half-damages or full damages? Full damages, since an ox can be expected to trample on anything that lies before him, and there is nothing unusual about such behaviour.

What if I leave my china tea-set in a public place, for instance, the High Street? If an ox now comes along and tramples on it, the ox's owner has no responsibility for the damage, since I had no business to leave my goods in a public place, and the ox is entitled to be there.

But suppose the ox, coming across my china tea-set in the High Street, instead of trampling on it, gores with his horns and prances off with a Wedgwood tea-cup transfixed on each horn? This is aggressive behaviour, and aggressive behaviour is always, to some extent, the responsibility of the ox's owner. Even though the responsibility is diminished by the unusual character of the damage, so that only half-damages need be paid (on the first two occasions of such damage), nevertheless this diminished responsibility applies even in a public place. If an animal shows any inclination to be aggressive, its owner ought to take precautions wherever the animal goes.

The question now arises, 'Suppose I place my china tea-set in my own field, and my neighbour's ox strays in and gores it with his horns?' Does the diminished responsibility (arising from unusual aggressive behaviour) still apply, or does the fact that the owner has allowed his animal to stray become the deciding factor, making him incur a penalty of full damages instead of half?

This is where the disagreement between Rabbi Tarfon and the Sages occurs. Rabbi Tarfon says that the deciding factor is the location of the damage; consequently the owner of the goring ox must pay full damages. The Sages say the deciding factor is the kind of damage; so the goring ox always incurs only half-damages.

128

Rabbi Tarfon tries to enforce his argument by an argument of formal logic, based on the Rabbinic theory of the *a fortiori* argument. The Sages, answering in kind, offer a refutation which is also based on the formal logic of the *a fortiori* argument. This is an aspect of Rabbinical discussion on which a whole treatise could be written. The interested reader is referred to *Essays on Talmudic Logic* by Louis Jacobs, and 'Logical Problems in Jewish Tradition' by Heinrich Guggenheimer in *Confrontations with Judaism*, edited by Philip Longworth. The Rabbis were pioneers in the formalization of legal logic, a subject not studied by Aristotle or the other Greek logicians.

The Christian reader has probably been thinking, 'What has all this got to do with religion?' The Talmud is a religious work, and nothing has been understood about the Talmud or about Judaism unless it is grasped that 'the ox that gored' and similar topics form an integral part of the Jewish religious consciousness. The tractate of the Talmud called Bava Kamma ('the First Gate') of which the above-discussed passage forms part, is traditionally used as the introduction of the young student to Talmudic studies. Countless generations of young Jews have wrestled with the subtle distinctions between different kinds of damage (Ox, Pit, Eating Animal, Fire) and have taken for granted that in doing so they are engaging in a religious experience. For underlying all these distinctions is the idea of *justice*, which can never remain an abstract idea, but must be clothed with the reality of life-situations in all their God-given complexity. Such study is conducted in an attitude of keen attention and intellectual enjoyment, with a cut-and-thrust of questions and objections. But it also has a ritual air, expressed in chanting. Every Talmudic argument-form has its own characteristic chant. Silent thought is not regarded as of much value even for someone studying alone. A student must sing his thoughts in order to get the swing of the argument. There is no set tune, but there is a supply of musical themes on which the student unconsciously improvises. To hear a Talmud student chanting his studies is to hear the music of Judaism. The message conveyed by it is that there is a mysticism of the intellect; that religious experience can arise from strenuous exercise of the mind, not, as Gentiles think, only from emptying the mind.

Arguing for Mastery

SEVEN VOWS AND SEVEN CUSHIONS

Rav Kahana was a disciple of Rav. One day an informer came into Rav's presence and was impudent to Rav. Upon this, Rav Kahana tore out the informer's windpipe.

Said Rav, 'Kahana, you will be sought by the Persian Government, so go to the Land of Israel. Moreover, I regard your act as somewhat blameworthy, so I impose on you this penalty. When you arrive in the Land of Israel, you will naturally attend the lectures of Rabbi Johanan, and you will wish to contribute to the discussion by raising objections to his arguments. But I order you not to raise any objection for seven years.'

When Rav Kahana arrived, he found Resh Lakish going over the subject-matter of the lecture of the next day with the younger Rabbis, to prepare them for the lecture. Rav Kahana pointed out some learned difficulties to Resh Lakish, who was so impressed that he went to Rabbi Johanan and said, 'A lion has come up from Babylon. Be careful.'

Next day, Rav Kahana was put into the first row of the disciples. But at the end of each stage of the lecture, he raised no difficulties, and at each stage he was moved back one row, untl he had been moved back seven rows.

Said Rabbi Johanan, 'The lion has turned out to be a fox.'

Then Rav Kahana prayed silently, 'May it be the will of Heaven that these seven rows should be accepted for the seven years.'

Then he stood up and asked that the lecture should be given again.

This time, after every stage of the lecture, Rav Kahana pointed out formidable difficulties. At each stage, he was moved one row up, until he was back in the first row.

Rabbi Johanan was unable to answer Rav Kahana's questions. At the beginning of the lecture, Rabbi Johanan was sitting on seven cushions. Every time he failed to solve a difficulty, one cushion was taken away, until in the end he was seated on the bare ground.

Rabbi Johanan was old, and his eyebrows overhung his eyes. He said, 'Lift up my eyebrows, so that I can see this man.'

Now, as it happened, Rav Kahana had a twisted lip which made him seem to be smiling. When Rabbi Johanan saw this, he thought that Rav Kahana was smiling in triumph. Rabbi Johanan gave him an involuntary glance of anger, and Rav Kahana immediately died.

It was then explained to Rabbi Johanan that Rav Kahana had a twisted lip which made him appear to smile. Rabbi Johanan was full of remorse. He went to the cave where Rav Kahana was buried, and found that a snake was coiled round it.

Said Rabbi Johanan, 'Snake, snake, release your tail from your mouth and let the master go in to visit his disciple.'

But the snake did not release its tail from its mouth.

Then Rabbi Johanan said, 'Snake, snake, release your tail from your mouth, and let the scholar go in to visit his colleague.'

Still the snake did not release his tail from his mouth.

Then Rabbi Johanan said, 'Snake, snake, release your tail from your mouth, and let the disciple go in to visit his master.'

Then the snake released his tail from his mouth, and allowed Rabbi Johanan to enter the cave. There he prayed to God, and raised Rav Kahana from death to life.

Bava Kamma, 117a

THE DEFEAT OF RABBI AKIVA

The following story concerns an argument between the great Rabbi Akiva and an unknown scholar called Jonathan. To our surprise, the famous Rabbi Akiva is ignominiously defeated in the argument, and has to flee in disgrace from the contest.

The subject of the argument is 'the daughter's co-wife'. Is a man allowed to marry his daughter's 'co-wife'?

The situation envisaged is this. Suppose a man marries his niece, the daughter of his brother (this is allowed in Jewish law). Suppose now that the man dies childless. We now have a piquant situation, because, in Jewish law, when a man dies childless, his brother is enjoined to marry the widow (this is called 'levirate' marriage, see Deuteronomy, 25: 5–10). In this case, the brother obviously cannot marry the widow, because she is his own daughter. But suppose that there is another widow: the dead man had two wives, neither of whom had a child. May he now marry his daughter's 'co-wife', or does the incest-ban extend to the 'co-wife' too, even though she is not his daughter? The majority opinion, championed by Rabbi Akiva, was that the 'daughter's co-wife' is forbidden. The minority opinion, championed by Jonathan, is that she is permitted.

In the days of Rabbi Dosa ben Hyrcanus, it became known that the people in his neighbourhood regarded it as permitted for a man to marry (by levirate marriage) the co-wife of his daughter. (This was the opinion of the House of Shammai, but the law had been decided by majority vote in favour of the contrary opinion of the House of Hillel.)

The Rabbis were troubled about this news, for Rabbi Dosa was a great man, and it would be awkward to have to discipline him. They could not speak to him directly, because the onset of blindness prevented him from attending the House of Study.

They said, 'And who will go and let him know?'

Said Rabbi Joshua, 'I will go.'

'And after him, who?'

'Rabbi Eleazar ben Azariah.'

'And after him. who?'

'Rabbi Akiva.'

The three rabbis journeyed to Rabbi Dosa's house, and stood by the door. Rabbi Dosa's maidservant went in and said to him, 'Rabbi, the Wise Men of Israel have come to visit you.'

He said to her, 'Let them enter.' And they entered.

Rabbi Dosa grasped Rabbi Joshua by the hand and seated him on a couch of gold.

132

Said Rabbi Joshua, 'Rabbi, tell your other pupil to sit.'

'Who is he?' asked Rabbi Dosa.

'Rabbi Eleazar ben Azariah.'

Said he, 'And has our comrade, Azariah, a son? Apply to him this verse: "I have been a young man, and I have also grown old, and I have not seen a righteous man forsaken and his seed seeking bread." ' And he seized Rabbi Eleazar by the hand and seated him on a couch of gold.

Said Rabbi Joshua, 'Rabbi, tell your other pupil to sit.'

'And who is he?'

'Akiva ben Joseph.'

He said to him, 'Are you Akiva ben Joseph, whose name goes from one end of the world to the other? Sit, my son, sit. May your like increase in Israel.'

They began to lead him on in the discussion of laws, until they reached the topic of 'the co-wife of the daughter'. They said to him, 'The co-wife of the daughter, what is her law?'

He said, 'It is a point of disagreement between the House of Shammai and the House of Hillel.'

'According to whom is the Halakha?'

He said, 'The Halakha is according to the House of Hillel.'

They said to him, 'Is it not said in your name that the Halakha is according to the House of Shammai?'

He said to them, 'Did you hear this said in the name of "Dosa" or in the name of "the son of Hyrcanus"?'

They said to him, 'By our life, Rabbi, we heard it inexplicitly.'

He said to them, 'I have a younger brother. He is the first-born of Satan, and his name is Jonathan. He is of the disciples of Shammai, and take care that he does not smite you with Halakhas, for he has three hundred reasons why the co-wife of the daughter is permitted. But I call to witness on my behalf the heavens and the earth that on this seat sat Haggai the prophet and said three things: the co-wife of the daughter is forbidden, Ammon and Moab set aside the Poor Man's Tithe in the Seventh Year,* and we may receive proselytes from the Cordyenians and the Tadmorites.'†

---

*Jews in Israel did not have to give any tithes in the Seventh Year, when the land had to lie fallow. But Jews in the neighbouring lands of Ammon and Moab, where there was no fallow year, were required to give tithes in the Seventh Year (by rabbinical ordinance). A question then arose about the Second Tithe (for

When they went in, they went in by one door, but when they went out they went out by three doors [in fear of meeting Jonathan]. Yet he (Jonathan) caught up with Rabbi Akiva and plied him with questions and defeated him in argument.

Said Jonathan, 'You are Akiva ben Joseph, whose name goes from one end of the world to the other. Happy are you that you have acquired a name. Yet you have still not reached the status of those who herd cattle.'

'No,' said Rabbi Akiva, 'not even to the status of those who herd sheep.'

Yevamot, 16a

Note. This story is a kind of analogue of the tale in Norse mythology, in which Thor, the strongest of the gods, meets an unknown stranger who contemptuously defeats him in a trial of strength. The Jewish heroes are intellectual heroes, priding themselves on their power of argument, but the story has the same moral: do not pride yourself on your greatness and fame, for the world contains resources that you know nothing of, and the strongest one of all may be one who cares nothing for fame. (Compare the story of Solomon, used by Kipling, in which Solomon, proud of his riches, prepares a feast for all the animals on land and sea. A huge creature appears from the depths of the ocean, swallows the whole meal in one mouthful, declares his disappointment with the quantity of food provided, and returns to the depths after explaining that he is the youngest and smallest of a hundred brothers.)

The end of the story is somewhat cryptic. The meaning may be this: the Rabbis were trying to impose discipline on all the Wise Men, even those mavericks like Jonathan who refused to obey

expenses of pilgrimages to Jerusalem) and the Poor Man's Tithe (to be given to the poor). These two tithes were given in Israel as follows: Second Tithe in the first, second, fourth and fifth years of the seven-year cycle; Poor Man's Tithe in the third and sixth year. Which of these two alternating tithes was to be given in Ammon and Moab in the Seventh Year? The matter is fully discussed in Mishnah Yadaim, 4:3. Ammon and Moab today form part of the Kingdom of Jordan, and its capital city Amman actually derives its name from the ancient name Ammon.

†There was some question whether these people were actually Jews by descent; if so, they did not require conversion in order to be accepted as Jews. The decision is thus they are not Jews and do require conversion if they wish to practise Judaism.

134

majority decisions. Jonathan says to Akiva: 'You cannot herd us Wise Men like cattle.' Akiva replies ruefully, 'I can't even herd sheep, never mind cattle', i.e. he has his difficulties even with lesser men than Jonathan. There is probably a reference to the fact that Akiva began his life as a shepherd.

The Limits of Argument

Rabbi Jose ben Taddai of Tiberias put the following *a fortiori* argument to Rabban Gamaliel: I am forbidden to marry my daughter, but my daughter's mother is permitted to me.

All the more so, then, I should be forbidden to marry the daughter of someone who is forbidden to me.

I am forbidden to marry somebody else's wife.'

Therefore, I should be forbidden to marry the daughter of somebody else's wife.

Therefore all marriages should be forbidden (except to the daughters of unmarried mothers, widows or divorcees).

For this argument, Rabban Gamaliel excommunicated Rabbi Jose ben Taddai (on the ground that he was bringing rabbinical methods of argument into discredit).

Derekh Eretz Rabba, 1

RABBI JEREMIAH GOES TOO FAR

'If a fledgling bird is found within fifty cubits of a dove-cote, it belongs to the owner of the dove-cote. If it is found outside the limit of fifty cubits, it belongs to the person who finds it' (Mishnah).

Rabbi Jeremiah asked the question: If one foot of the fledgling is within the limit of fifty cubits, and one foot is outside it, what is the law?

It was for this question that Rabbi Jeremiah was thrown out of the House of Study.

Bava Batra, 23b

136

Food which has been removed from a hot-plate on the Sabbath may be returned to it, but only if the remover has kept the food in his hand, not if he has set it down on the ground.

Rabbi Jeremiah asked the question: 'What if he hung it up on a stick?'

Shabbat, 38b

Rabbi Meir says: 'If a woman gave birth to a deformed child in the shape of an animal, she still counts legally as a woman who has borne a child.' The Sages, however, ruled: 'Anything that has not the shape of a human being cannot be regarded as a human child' (Mishnah).

Rabbi Jeremiah enquired of Rabbi Zera: 'According to Rabbi Meir, what if the father had arranged a betrothal for a female creature thus born? And what difference could that make? It would make a difference in that the betrothed man might be legally barred from marrying its sister. . . .'

Rabbi Aha ben Jacob said: 'Rabbi Zera never laughed in his life, and even Rabbi Jeremiah failed to make him laugh.'

Niddah, 23a

Note. The great scholar Isaac Halevi in his Dorot Ha-rishonim *(pp. 364ff) tried to argue that all Rabbi Jeremiah's questions were meant seriously, being intended to attack the Sages' methods of fixing limits and measures. Significantly, however, Halevi makes no reference to the last-given instance above, or to the comment of Rabbi Aha ben Jacob.*

Corn which has grown to a third of its full size at the time of the New Year belongs to the previous year for purposes of the rules of the Seventh Year and tithing.

Said Rabbi Jeremiah to Rabbi Zera: 'How were the Rabbis so certain about this distinction between a third and less than a third?'

Said Rabbi Zera: 'How many times have I told you not to

put yourself outside the established rule? All the measurements of the Sages are like this. A ritual bath may be taken in 40 Seahs of water; but if the water is less than 40 Seahs by a tiny quantity, it is not valid for a ritual bath. If food is equal to the size of an egg, it can become unclean; but if it is one grain short of that size, it cannot become unclean. . . .'

Said Rabbi Jeremiah: 'What I said was worthless.'

Note. This exchange suggests that the trouble with Rabbi Jeremiah was that he was an ultra-rationalist, who could not bring himself to accept the element of arbitrariness in human affairs. His teacher, Rabbi Zera, tried to reconcile him to the fact that rules have to be precise, even though no reason can be given why the line is drawn precisely at this point.

Rabbi Jeremiah was eventually accepted back into the House of Study, and, in time, became a great authority.

The next passage shows him applying his capacity for asking ingenious questions in a more acceptable manner.

If a man dies leaving sons and daughters, the distribution of the estate depends on whether it is large or small. If it is large, the sons inherit and the daughters are maintained until they marry. If it is small, it is used to maintain the daughters, and the sons can go begging.

Rabbi Jeremiah sat before Rabbi Abbahu and asked him the following question:

' (a) If there is a widow, can her allowance reduce the estate from a "large" one to a "small" one (so bringing it about that the sons receive nothing), or does she have no priority (in view of the fact that her maintenance is conditional on her remaining unmarried), so that the estate remains a "large" one, the sons inherit and provide for both widow and daughters?

(b) If the answer to (a) is that the widow does not have priority, does a step-daughter have priority? On the one hand, her maintenance continues even if she marries, but on the other she does not transmit the obligation to her heirs if she dies.

(c) If the answer to (b) is that the step-daughter does not have priority, does a creditor have priority (thus having the capability of reducing a "large" estate to a "small" estate)? On the one hand, he does transmit the obligation to his heirs, but on the other hand, the debt still requires collecting. . . .'

Said Rabbi Abbahu: 'Go away today and come back tomorrow.'

Refuting Unbelievers

THE HUMP-BACKED SAGE

Gebiha ben Pesisa was a Sage who was hump-backed.

A Sadducee said to him, 'Woe to you wicked ones who say that the dead will be brought back to life. If people already alive die, how can people who have died come to life?'

He replied, 'Woe to you wicked ones who say that the dead will not be brought back to life. If those who did not exist at all now live, shall not those who have lived live again?'

Said the Sadducee, 'You have called me wicked. I have a good mind to stand up and kick off your hump.'

Said Gebiha, 'If you could do that, you could set up as a doctor and command large fees.'

Sanhedrin, 91a

THE CENTRE OF THE EARTH

When Rabbi Joshua ben Hanania went to Athens to dispute with the philosophers there, they asked him many questions and he answered them all successfully.

One of their questions was, 'Where is the centre of the earth?'

Rabbi Joshua pointed with his forefinger to a spot on the ground nearby, and said, 'Here.'

Said they, 'How do we know that you are right?'

Said he, 'Bring your measuring-rods, and measure it for yourselves.'

Bekhorot, 8b

140

Arguing with God*

THE DAY GOD LAUGHED

On that day, Rabbi Eliezer put forward all the arguments in the world, but the Sages did not accept them.

Finally, he said to them, 'If the *halakhah* is according to me, let that carob-tree prove it.'

He pointed to a near-by carob-tree, which then moved from its place a hundred cubits, and some say, four hundred cubits.

They said to him, 'One cannot bring a proof from the moving of a carob-tree.'

Said Rabbi Eliezer, 'If the *halakhah* is according to me, may that stream of water prove it.'

The stream of water then turned and flowed in the opposite direction.

They said to him, 'One cannot bring a proof from the behaviour of a stream of water.'

Said Rabbi Eliezer, 'If the *halakhah* is according to me, may the walls of the House of Study prove it.'

The walls of the House of Study began to bend inwards. Rabbi Joshua then rose up and rebuked the walls of the House of Study. 'If the students of the Wise argue with one another in *halakhah*,' he said, 'what right have you to interfere?'

In honour of Rabbi Joshua, the walls ceased to bend inwards; but in honour of Rabbi Eliezer, they did not straighten up, and they remain bent to this day.

Then said Rabbi Eliezer to the Sages, 'If the *halakhah* is according to me, may a proof come from Heaven.'

*See also 'Accepting Majority Decisions'.

Then a heavenly voice went forth, and said, 'What have you to do with Rabbi Eliezer? The *halakhah* is according to him in every place.'

Then Rabbi Joshua rose up on his feet, and said, 'It is not in the heavens [Deuteronomy, 30: 12].'

What did he mean by quoting this? Said Rabbi Jeremiah, 'He meant that since the Torah has been given already on Mount Sinai, we do not pay attention to a heavenly voice; for Thou hast written in Thy Torah, "Decide according to the majority" [Exodus, 23: 2].'

Rabbi Nathan met the prophet Elijah. He asked him, 'What was the Holy One, blessed be He, doing in that hour?'

Said Elijah, 'He was laughing, and saying, "My children have defeated me, my children have defeated me." '

Bava Metsia, 59b

Note. This extraordinary story strikes the key-note of the Talmud. God is a good Father, who wants his children to grow up and achieve independence. He has given them His Torah, but now wants them to develop it in their own way. Yet this is not an out-and-out humanism, in which God is rejected and the miraculous is altogether discounted. The divine and the miraculous exist, but they must give way to the demands of human discussion and rationality.

This profound story was dismissed as one of the 'imbecilities' of the Talmud in the medieval Disputation of Paris, when the Talmud was put on trial by Christians.

THE EXCOMMUNICATION OF RABBI ELIEZER

Since Rabbi Eliezer refused to retract his opinion, despite the majority vote against him, it was decided to excommunicate him. But Rabbi Eliezer was a figure of such spiritual power that to excommunicate him was a dangerous undertaking. Even though he accepted his sentence of excommunication with humility, emanations of grief or displeasure from such a man could cause upheavals in nature and prove dangerous to the Rabbis who had voted for his excommunication, and especially for Rabban Gamaliel, the President of the Council.

Then they took a vote, and excommunicated him.

Then they said, 'Who will go and tell him?'

Rabbi Akiva said to them, 'I will go. For if some unfit person should go and tell him, the result may be the destruction of the entire world.'

What did Rabbi Akiva do?

He put on black clothes, and wrapped himself all in black, and went to Rabbi Eliezer, and sat down four cubits away from him.

Rabbi Eliezer said to him, 'Akiva, how is this day different from other days?'

Rabbi Akiva said to him, 'Master, it appears to me that your companions are separating themselves from you.'

Then Rabbi Eliezer rent his garments, took off his shoes, left his chair, and sat on the earth, in accordance with the law of an excommunicated man.

The tears began to flow from Rabbi Eliezer's eyes, and the world began to suffer: a third of the olive crop, a third of the wheat, and a third of the barley crop, withered. Some say: even the dough in the hands of the kneading women was spoilt. And any place on which Rabbi Eliezer cast his eyes was burnt up.

Also, Rabban Gamaliel, who was travelling in a ship at that time, came into great peril from a huge wave which suddenly arose and threatened to drown him.

Said Rabban Gamaliel, 'It seems to me that this can only be because of Rabbi Eliezer.'

So he stood on his feet, and said, 'Master of the Universe, it is known and revealed before Thee that not for my glory did I act, nor for the glory of my father's house, but for Thy glory, and for the unity of Israel.'

On this, the sea subsided from its rage.

Bava Metsia, 59b

THE DEATH OF RABBI ELIEZER

When Rabbi Eliezer became fatally ill, Rabbi Akiva and his colleagues went to visit him. He was sitting up in his four-poster bed, and they sat down in the outer room.

143

That day was the eve of the Sabbath, and Hyrcanus, Rabbi Eliezer's son, went in to take off his father's phylacteries.

Rabbi Eliezer sharply rebuked his son, who came out in confusion, and said to his companions, 'I think that Father's mind is unclear.'

Rabbi Eliezer, hearing this, said to the Rabbis, 'It is he and his mother whose minds are unclear. Why are they neglecting a duty which involves a punishment of stoning in order to attend to a duty which is a mere rabbinical enactment?'

When the Rabbis saw that his mind was in good order, they entered and sat before him at a distance of four cubits.

He said to them, 'Why have you come?'

Said they, 'We have come to learn Torah.'

He said to them, 'And until now, why did you not come?'

Said they, 'We did not have time.'

Said he, 'I doubt whether they will die a natural death.'

Rabbi Akiva said to him, 'What will be my death?'

He said to him, 'Your death will be even worse than theirs.'

Then he folded his two arms over his heart, and said, 'Woe to you, my two arms, which are like two rolled-up scrolls of the Law. Much Torah have I learnt, and much Torah have I taught. But I only skimmed of the knowledge of my teachers, like a dog licking from the sea; and my pupils have only skimmed of my knowledge, like one who dips the stick into the paint-tube. I know three hundred laws about the "intensely bright spot" of leprosy, and no one has ever asked me about them. Moreover, I know three hundred laws [some say, three thousand laws] about the planting of cucumbers, and no one has ever asked me about them—except Akiva ben Joseph. Once, he and I were walking on the road, and he said to me, "My teacher, teach me about the planting of cucumbers." I said one word, and the whole field became filled with cucumbers. He said to me, "My teacher, you have taught me their planting; now teach me their removal." I said one word, and the cucumbers were all gathered into one place.'

The Rabbis said to him, 'What is the law about a leather ball, and about a shoe-maker's leather last, and about an amulet, and about a piece of leather in which jewels are bound up, and about a small leather-covered weight? Are they susceptible of uncleanness?'

He said to them, 'Yes, they are susceptible, and they may be purified just as they are.'

'What is the law about a shoe which is upon the last?'

'It is clean.' And with the word 'clean', his soul departed.

Rabbi Joshua stood on his feet and said, 'The vow is released; the vow is released.'

On the expiration of the Sabbath, Rabbi Akiva met the funeral procession as it went from Caesarea to Lydda, and he struck his own body until the blood flowed to the ground. He made a funeral oration before the line of mourners, saying, ' "My father, my father, the chariot of Israel and the horsemen thereof!" [II Kings, 2: 12]. I have many coins, but there is no money-changer to assort them.'

Sanhedrin, 68a

Notes. The phylacteries: *these are not worn on the Sabbath, but Rabbi Eliezer thought his son should be seeing to more important things, such as the lighting of the Sabbath lights. If these are lit too late, when the Sabbath has actually begun, a serious infringement of the Sabbath is involved.*

Four cubits: *Rabbi Eliezer could not be approached more closely, because he was still under excommunication for refusing to accept the majority decision of the Rabbis on various matters on which he disagreed with them.*

Cucumbers: *these laws concerned witchcraft, which was forbidden, except in the way of demonstration when expounding its laws.*

Leather ball, etc.: *these were some of the matters which led to Rabbi Eliezer's excommunication. Leather articles were susceptible to ritual uncleanness only if they were in the shape of a receptacle. But what if the receptacle was intended to be stuffed with wool or hair? In that case, they did not count as receptacles, according to the Rabbis, but Rabbi Eliezer disagreed, and stuck to his disagreement up to his last breath.*

The shoe on the last: *this is a different point of disagreement. Manufactured articles were susceptible to uncleanness only when the work of their manufacture was complete. Was a shoe complete when all that required to be done was to remove it from the last, a task that could be performed by an unskilled person? The Rabbis said 'Yes', but Rabbi Eliezer said 'No'.*

The vow is released: *the excommunication is at an end.*

I have many coins, etc.: *I have many questions to ask, but no one to resolve them.*

'I doubt whether they will die a natural death': *many of the Rabbis who congregated at Rabbi Eliezer's death-bed were executed cruelly by the Romans after the revolt of Bar Kochba (132–135 CE). Rabbi Akiva died the cruellest death of all, being flayed alive with iron combs. The suggestion is that this was partly due to their treatment of Rabbi Eliezer—not that they were wrong to excommunicate him for his obstinacy, but his* mana *was so great that even to punish him justly was dangerous.*

SEND FOR RABBAH BAR NAHMANI

One day, they were disputing in the Heavenly Academy about the laws of leprosy. It was agreed that if the bright spot precedes the white hair, the man is unclean. It was also agreed that if the white hair precedes the bright spot, the man is clean. They disagreed, however, about the case where the order of appearance is in doubt. The Holy One, blessed be He, was of the opinion that the man is clean. The rest of the Heavenly Academy were of the opinion that the man is unclean.

'To whom shall we submit the matter?' they asked, and answered, 'To Rabbah bar Nahmani, who, as he himself has declared, is the unique authority on the laws of leprosy and tents.'*

So they sent the Angel of Death to summon Rabbah bar Nahmani to the Heavenly Academy, and that is how he came to die so young.

Bava Metsia, 86a

Note. This daring story is one of the 'blasphemies' of the Talmud listed in the charge-sheet of the Paris Disputation of 1240. A human being has made himself such an authority on a section of the Law that God Himself has to consult him about it. Note that

---

*A technical word. See Numbers, 19: 14: 'This is the law when a man dieth in a tent: all that come into the tent and all that is in the tent shall be unclean seven days.' The detailed definition of a 'tent', or 'overshadowing object', was a complicated matter requiring expert knowledge such as that of Rabbah bar Nahmani.

146

God does not attempt to overrule the Heavenly Academy. God has been 'rabbinized', and the dictum, 'The Torah is not in heaven' becomes the watchword of rabbinical humanism.

THE MAN WHO BLACKMAILED GOD—HONI THE CIRCLE-MAKER

Once they said to Honi the Circle-maker, 'Pray for rain'. He said, 'Do not leave any clay ovens in the open air, in case they should melt when the rains come down.'

However, when he prayed, the rain did not fall. What did he do? He drew a circle and stood within it and said before God, 'Lord of the Universe, thy children have turned their faces towards me, for I am like a son of thy household. I swear by Thy great Name that I shall not move from here until thou hast mercy on thy children.'

The rain began to fall drop by drop. Said Honi, 'I did not ask for this, but for rain that will fill the cisterns, pits and caverns.'

It began to rain violently. Said Honi, 'I did not ask for this, but for rain of good will, blessing and graciousness.'

It now rained steadily at the right volume, until Israel went out of Jerusalem to the Temple Mount before the rains. They came and said to him, 'Just as you prayed that rain should come, so pray now that it will stop.'

He said to them, 'Go out and see if the Stone of Loss has been covered.'

Simeon ben Shetah sent to him, saying, 'If you were not Honi, I would have excommunicated you. But what shall I do to you? You tease God, yet he performs your will, like a son who teases his father, who yet performs his will.'

Mishnah, Ta'anit, 3: 8

Note. This story, from an earlier period, shows a very different kind of wrestling with God. Honi, the charismatic wonder-worker, almost dares God to refuse his prayer. He stages a sit-in strike until his prayer is granted. He is like a spoilt child, who trades on his father's affection for him by putting himself into a situation where a refusal would be so humiliating that his father does not have the heart to refuse. This is really a situation of utter dependence—but there is a kind of power in such dependence.

This is at the opposite extreme to the Rabbis who wrestle with God in order to exercise the independence which they know He wishes to grant them. Simeon ben Shetah, representing the rationalistic Rabbis, disapproves of Honi's conduct, yet half-admires Honi's closeness to God and daring faith, which allows him to take such risks. Two approaches to God are here exemplified, both of which exist in Judaism and are held in tension, though the rationalistic approach is dominant.

HYGIENE

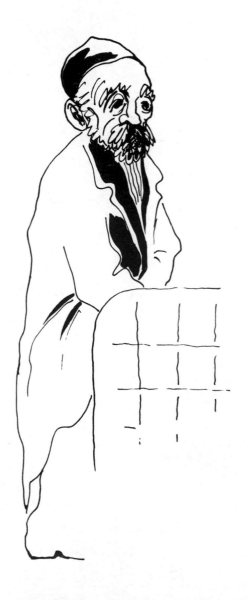

Privy-Etiquette

Said Rabbi Akiva: 'Once I followed Rabbi Joshua into a privy and I learnt from him three things:

1. I learnt that one does not place one self east and west, but north and south;

2. I learnt that one does not defecate standing but sitting;

3. and I learnt that one does not wipe with the right hand but with the left.'

Ben Azai said to him, 'To such a point did you brazen your face to your teacher?'

He said to him, 'It is Torah, and I have to learn.'

Berakhot, 62a

151

Dangers of Delaying Urination

The Rabbis once said to Rabbi Abba ben Zavda, 'Take a wife and beget children.'

He replied, 'If I had been worthy to have children, I would have had them by my first wife.'

However, this was just an evasion, for the truth was that Rabbi Abba ben Zavda became impotent through the long discourses of Rabbi Huna. The same thing happened to Rabbi Giddal, Rabbi Helbo, and Rabbi Shesheth: they were all too polite to urinate, and so lost their potency.

Rabbi Aha ben Jacob said, 'We were a group of sixty scholars, and all became impotent because of the long discourses of Rabbi Huna, except myself, who followed the principle, "Wisdom preserveth the life of him that hath it" ' [Ecclesiastes, 7: 12].

Yevamot, 64b

HEALTH BEFORE DECORUM

Rabbi Abba ben Hiyya ben Abba said in the name of Rabbi Johanan: 'It is permitted to urinate in public, but not to drink water in public.'

It once happened that someone delayed in urinating, and his belly became swollen.

Samuel needed to urinate while discoursing on a Sabbath preceding a festival. He spread his cloak as a screen between his audience and himself.

He came before his father, who said, 'I will give you four

152

hundred zuz to announce that this act of yours was not necessary, for someone who did not have a cloak might delay and expose himself to danger.'

Mar son of Ashi was walking near a landing-bridge when he needed to ease himself. Someone said to him, 'Your mother-in-law is coming.' He replied, 'I would do it even in her ear.'

Our Rabbis taught: 'Two channels are in the membrum, one of which discharges urine and the other semen, and the distance between them is no more than the peel of garlic. If a person delays urinating, and one channel obstructs the other, he becomes impotent.'

Bekhorot, 44b

LECTURES ON HYGIENE

Rav Huna said to his son Rabbah, 'Why do you not frequent Rav Hisda, whose discourse is so keen?'

Said Rabbah, 'Why should I go to him? When I go to him, he discourses on worldly matters.'

'What wordly things?'

'That a person who enters a privy should not sit down abruptly, and should not force himself to defecate, because the rectum is supported by three teeth-like glands, and if they are dislocated by over-forcing, there is danger to life.'

Said Rav Huna, 'Rav Hisda is dealing with matters which are vital to the life of the created beings, and you say that they are worldly matters! I am now all the more convinced that you should go to him.'

Shabbat, 82a

Uncovered Liquids

Priestly wine which was left uncovered should be poured away; and it goes without saying, that this applies to ordinary wine too. Three kinds of liquid are forbidden once they have been left uncovered: water, wine and milk. All other liquids are permitted. How long must they have remained uncovered to become forbidden? Long enough for a snake to come out from some nearby place and drink.

Mishnah, Terumot, 8: 4

Note. This is not 'ritual purity' law, but a matter of hygiene. Any liquid that might be attractive to a snake had to be kept covered, in case the snake's venom entered the liquid. There was one sect among the Pharisees, called the Hasidim, who thought that such precautions showed lack of faith in God. The Hasidim criticised only the hygienic *laws of the Rabbis, not the 'ritual purity' laws, which had a Scriptural basis. There is some evidence that Jesus belonged to the Hasidim.*

'Ritual Purity'

BURYING A CORPSE

A High Priest or a Nazarite are forbidden to become unclean by contact with a corpse even if it is the corpse of a close relative. However, if either of them comes across an unburied, neglected corpse, he must perform the duty of burying it, even though he becomes unclean thereby.

Suppose a High Priest and a Nazarite are walking along the road and they see an unburied, neglected corpse. Which of them should bury it? Rabbi Eliezer says: 'The High Priest'; but the Sages say: 'The Nazarite'.

Said Rabbi Eliezer, 'Let the High Priest bury it, for he does not have to bring a sacrifice to be purified of his uncleanness.'

Said the Sages, 'Let the Nazarite bury it, for his holiness is only temporary.'

Mishnah, Nazir, 7: 1

Note. 'Ritual purity' is one of the most difficult and complicated topics in the Talmud. It should not be confused with the Talmudic laws of hygiene, which have a rational, physiological basis. One can become ritually 'unclean' not only by touching a corpse, but even by being under the same roof as one. Other sources of ritual 'uncleanness' are a menstruating woman, a dead 'creeping thing', and a person suffering from gonorrhea. Also a lesser degree of uncleanness is incurred simply by having sexual intercourse, even though having such intercourse is regarded as a religious duty for husband and wife. Thus, 'uncleanness' is not a sinful state; on the contrary, most people are expected to be 'unclean' in some degree most of the time. When entering the Temple, however, or eating holy food at Festival time, one was required to take steps to be 'clean', which was accomplished by taking a ritual bath or baptism. The Priests, who were constantly in the Temple and eating holy food, had to be more careful than others to be 'clean'; and they were the only people who were actually forbidden to incur 'uncleanness' through a corpse (except that Nazarites, during the period of their vows, were subject to the same prohibition). An ordinary Priest was allowed to attend the funeral of a close relative, but not a High Priest. However, so important was the duty of burying an unburied, neglected corpse, that even a High Priest was obliged to incur 'uncleanness' in order to do so.

'Uncleanness' was regarded as a kind of invisible dirtiness, which had to be washed off before approaching holy areas or foodstuffs, just as one would wash off visible dirtiness before eating ordinary food. One could not help incurring this invisible dirtiness and was not blamed in the least for it, since the ordinary process of living (including the performance of religious duties) inevitably brought about 'uncleanness' (just as, on the visible plane, doing one's job as a farm labourer or factory hand is bound to make one dirty). All the kinds of invisible dirtiness are laid down in the Bible quite explicitly, so there was no possibility of ignoring the matter, even though the Rabbis were unable to give a rational explanation of it. But in their usual methodical way, they systematized the various degrees of 'uncleanness' and spent so much ingenuity on this that many commentators have over-estimated the importance of the topic in Judaism, and have failed to realize that for most of the people most of the time, 'uncleanness' did not have to be a matter of concern at all. After the destruction of the Temple, the whole topic eventually became a dead letter, since there were no longer any holy foodstuffs or areas that could be contaminated.

HOW TO HELP

Charity

THE RABBI AND THE SCHNORRER

A man once came before Rava and asked that he should be maintained at the public expense. Rava asked him, 'What kind of food do you eat?'

Said the man, 'I only eat fat chicken and old wine.'

Said Rava, 'Consider the burden you are putting on the community by eating such expensive food.'

Said the man, 'Do I eat of theirs? I eat the food of the All-Merciful, who provides for every individual in accordance with his own habits of eating.'

Just then, Rava's sister, who had not seen him for thirteen years, arrived and brought him a fat chicken and old wine.

Said the man, 'Isn't that just what I said?'

Said Rava, 'I apologise to you. Come and eat.'

Ketuvot, 67b

Note. This seems like an early version of a well-known Yiddish joke. A man gives a 'schnorrer' (Jewish beggar) some money. An hour later, to his surprise, he finds the 'schnorrer' sitting next to him at an expensive restaurant eating caviare. He expostulates, 'I thought you were supposed to be penniless. What are you doing eating caviare?' Says the 'schnorrer', 'I was penniless. But consider. If I have no money, I can't eat caviare. If someone gives me money, according to you I still shouldn't eat caviare. So when do I get to eat caviare?'

159

It is better for a man to skin animal carcases than to say to the community: 'Support me, I am a great sage.'

Bava Batra, 110a

Said Rabbi Joshua ben Hananiah: 'The poor do more for the rich man by accepting charity than the rich man does for the poor by bestowing it.'

Vayikra Rabbah, 34: 10

It is forbidden to cross a road to meet a man who is your debtor, and who you know cannot pay you; for it is as if he were tortured with fire and water.

Berakhot, 6b

There are eight degrees in charity, in ascending order.

The highest degree of all is to 'strengthen the hand' of the poor man, either by a gift or a loan or a partnership, in such a way that he has no need of further charity.

Next, is to give charity in such a way that the giver does not know to whom he has given and the receiver does not know from whom he has received.

Next, is to give charity in such a way that the giver knows to whom he has given, but the receiver does not know from whom he has received.

Next, is to give in such a way that the receiver knows from whom he has received but the giver does not know to whom he has given; for example, to throw a bag of money behind one, and not look to see which poor man took it, in case he should feel ashamed.

Next, is to give to the poor man into his hand before he asks for it.

Next, is to give to him after he has asked for it.

Next, is to give less than is fitting, but with a cheerful countenance.

160

Worst of all, is to give even a large amount, but with a grudging countenance.

Maimonides, Mishneh Torah, 'Seeds', II, 10 (summary)

A CONVERSATION ON CHARITY

MANKOWITZ   'Said Rabbi Joshua ben Hananiah: "The poor do more for the rich man by accepting charity than the rich man does for the poor man by bestowing it." ' Does this mean that the rich man needs a kind of lancing of his riches in order to retain his humanity, or is there a more specific, less psychological reason for it?

MACCOBY   The simple reason that the rabbi himself would have given is that the deed of giving charity is one of such importance that the poor man confers a great benefit on the rich man by enabling him to perform this good deed.

MANKOWITZ   But how would you define the benefit that the rich man receives by performing the good deed of charity? Does he receive a specific reward in this world? Or only in the World to Come?

MACCOBY   Certainly in the World to Come, but not necessarily in this world, as far as the individual is concerned. But society as a whole will benefit even in this world.

MANKOWITZ   Good deeds would set up vibrations that affect nature?

MACCOBY   Yes, everything would come right. For example, Hezekiah was a good king, and promoted deeds of charity among all his people; so the harvests were huge at that time, and all the fruit was about ten times bigger than at other times.

MANKOWITZ   Currently there must be a shortage of people doing good deeds. But you are still talking about long-term benefits which may or may not affect the person who does the good deed of charity. The World to Come is hardly discussed at all. It can be hoped for and worked for, but it can't

161

be discussed. And the material benefit of society at large is rather a remote aim too. But the possibility that the good deed, the act of charity in this case, done in this world, has a specific value, psychological, say, or spiritual, for the doer, is examinable and discussable. What did they say about that?

MACCOBY   There is a saying in the Mishnah—in the Ethics of the Fathers—that 'the reward of a good deed is another good deed',—that is to say, that if a man performs a good deed, God, as a reward, gives him the opportunity to perform another good deed. This is really the last word on the subject; it means that a good deed is its own reward. This is the way the rabbis felt about it: the greatest happiness was to be given an opportunity to fulfil a *mitzvah*, that is, something commanded by God in the Torah. Such opportunities may not occur as often as one would like. For example, there is the story, included in this anthology, of the rabbi who made a great feast of joy, because chance had put in his way the opportunity to do a certain good deed which he might have gone through the whole of his life and never had the chance to perform. The Bible says that if you are reaping your field and you forget a sheaf, you must leave it behind for the poor. This man said, 'I am not a forgetful person, yet for once in my life I did forget a sheaf. This is probably the only time in my life that I'll be able to perform this good deed.' So he made a great feast of thanksgiving and celebration.

MANKOWITZ   He inadvertently tricked himself into an act of love?

MACCOBY   Yes, he may have worked unconsciously for such an act of forgetfulness. One can imagine him sorrowfully collecting the last sheaf, time after time, and cursing his own relentless awareness, until one day, the blessed moment of forgetfulness came. Not that he would refrain from giving sheaves of corn to the poor anyway—but that would be ordinary, everyday charity, not the fulfilling of the holy precept of 'the forgotten sheaf', which could be fulfilled only through a genuine act of forgetfulness.

MANKOWITZ   Do you think that this has anything to do with what our Christian neighbours call love? Or is it a matter of chalking up another good deed to one's credit?

MACCOBY   It could decline into a matter of accountancy, or perhaps a collector's passion for adding one more good deed to one's collection. I don't think that it was often felt like that, because behind it all was the basic commandment, 'Thou shalt love thy neighbour as thyself.' The question was always how one could best express this love in practical terms. Love is not something that one feels, but something that one does.

MANKOWITZ   Surely I seem to remember somewhere that there is an idea that a *mitzvah* that is advertised, or publicized, ceases to have much value as a good deed?

MACCOBY   It's not so much a question of avoiding advertising, but of doing a good deed, an act of charity, in such a way that the person who receives the benefit is not humiliated. There is no harm in a person getting some kind of glory for doing good deeds, but if he gets the glory at the expense of the self-respect of the person to whom he's done the good deed, then it counts as a bad deed.

MANKOWITZ   So you shouldn't do a good act to someone in such a way as to mortify him by reminding of his need for that deed?

MACCOBY   That's exactly it.

MANKOWITZ   That's why so many hands that feed people get bitten—because of the manner in which they do the feeding.

MACCOBY   Yes, indeed. So much is this taken to heart in Talmudic Judaism, that it is considered that the

163

best way of doing charity is to convey one's gift to the person in need without even revealing one's identity. Even better than that is not to give, but to lend; because a person who borrows money preserves his self-respect in receiving a loan rather than a gift. In many Jewish communities, rich men will hand in money to the rabbi, to be distributed as gifts or loans to anyone in the community who needs it, on condition that the name of the donor is not to be revealed. Traditionally, it has been one of the functions of a rabbi to distribute such funds.

MANKOWITZ   My father was very strong on this kind of thing. He died recently, and on going through his papers, I found endless gifts and donations—things I didn't know he was involved in—things he didn't want anyone to know about, all sorts of funny, strange things.

MACCOBY   The Lady Bountiful who goes around scattering money to the poor—this isn't a Jewish ideal. She does it for herself, because it makes her feel good. On the contrary, the Jewish beggar, or *schnorrer*, tends to think that he is showing benevolence to the rich men who support him. A good many Jewish jokes are based on this idea —on the fact that a *schnorrer* usually feels very little need for gratitude to his benefactors. For example, the *schnorrer* to whom Rothschild (the archetypal giver in *schnorrer* stories) gave £5 instead of the usual £10, explaining that he had had great expenses recently, as he had made an expensive wedding for his daughter. Says the *schnorrer*, 'At my expense you are marrying your daughter?'

MANKOWITZ   In Islam too, the beggar never gives thanks to the donor, but to Allah. And the donor is expected to give thanks to Allah that he has the superfluous wherewithal to give charity to the beggar.

MACCOBY   That is a very similar attitude. Perhaps there is

this difference—that in Judaism, there are no holy beggars. The *schnorrer* is not a holy man, but a man of *chutzpah*, who takes advantage of the position which the laws of charity give him. To be a parasite on society is never a position of respect.

MANKOWITZ Yes, here is a saying that bears that out: 'It is better for a man to skin animal carcasses'—what a filthy activity; if you've ever flayed an animal, you really know what that means—'than to say to the community, "Support me, I am a great sage." ' Some of these sayings are so good, you can really live by them. This saying, I take it, relates to that general principle that the rabbis maintained, that a rabbi should also keep a small shop, practise a craft, and so on.

MACCOBY Yes, ideally a rabbi is an unpaid lay-leader, who has his own profession. Among the rabbis of the Talmud was one who was a shoemaker—Johanan ha-sandlar. The great Hillel was a wood-cutter, and Shammai was a carpenter. Jesus was a rabbi and a carpenter, and there was nothing unusual about this—so the New Testament story that people despised him for being a carpenter is inauthentic. Famous medieval rabbis such as Maimonides and Nachmanides were physicians. Eventually, however, the Jews degenerated to the point where being a rabbi was a profession just as it is in other religions. In Islam, one should say, there is the same ideal of the unpaid religious leader, and the same degeneration.

MANKOWITZ One can at least say, in favour of the rabbis, that they are very badly paid. But here is another saying which has some bearing on what you were saying about the way charity should be given: 'It is forbidden to cross a road to meet a man who is your debtor, and who you know cannot pay you, for it is as if he were tortured with fire and water.'

MACCOBY This is an example of the delicacy which is one of

165

the characteristics of the Talmud. In some ways, the Talmud can be regarded as gross—I mean by puritanic Victorian standards. But in some ways —far more important ways—the Talmud is very, very delicate. It's very concerned about sparing people's feelings. To embarrass or shame someone is called in Hebrew 'to make his face white in public', and the Talmud, by a play on words, says that this is as bad as to shed blood. In this case, to bring it into the open that a person owes one money which he cannot pay, is 'to make his face white in public', and one should therefore forego the usual courtesy of crossing the road to greet him—one should pretend that one has not seen him, and this apparent discourtesy is the true politeness. Another example of misplaced courtesy is mentioned in the Talmud: if an enemy or rival has suffered a great loss, one should not go immediately to comfort him, as he will feel that one is gloating over him, even if that is not one's intention. One must have the delicacy to think, 'Poor fellow, I know he is in trouble; and I am the last person he wants to see just now.'

MANKOWITZ   It is a recognition, isn't it, of the psychological need that human beings have for dignity, for *amour propre*, self-respect.

MACCOBY   And also a kind of realism by which it is realized that being saintly, or putting on an air of saintliness, is a way of aggression against people; that sometimes you can be charitable in a way that is an attack. Judaism acknowledges that there are people who hate one another, or who feel great rivalry with each other. One must show love for one's enemy or rival, but not in a way that pretends that the enmity does not exist, or which carries on the war under a cloak of charitableness. One must not, for example, forgive people in a way which makes them feel like kicking one in the face. Forgiveness must not be used as an

166

instrument of one-upmanship; even if this is actually not one's intention, but only the way it is bound to seem to the person involved.

THE FORGOTTEN SHEAF

It happened with a certain Hasid that he forgot to gather a sheaf of corn which was standing in his field.

He said to his son, 'Go and sacrifice for me a bull for a burnt-offering, and another bull for a peace-offering.'

Said his son, 'Father, why do you see fit to rejoice over this duty [i.e. the duty of leaving the Forgotten Sheaf for the poor: see Deuteronomy, 24: 19: "When thou reapest thy harvest in thy field, and has forgot a sheaf in the field, thou shalt not go back to fetch it; it shall be for the stranger, for the fatherless and for the widow"] more than over all the other duties of the Torah?'

Said his father, 'All the other duties of the Torah come to us by paying attention, but this one comes to us by inattention. All the earnestness and good intentions in the world will not bring us the merit of this deed, only a moment of forgetfulness.'

Tosefta, Peah, 3

Regard for Feelings

THE SMELL OF GARLIC

It once happened that while Rabbi was delivering a lecture he noticed a smell of garlic.

He then said, 'Let him who has eaten garlic go out.'

Rabbi Hiyya arose and left; not because he had eaten garlic, but because he wished to save the offender from humiliation.

However, when the other disciples saw Rabbi Hiyya go out, each of them in turn rose up and went out.

Sanhedrin, 11a

CELEBRATING THE BRIDE

How does one sing when dancing before the bride? The House of Shammai say, 'One sings her praises without overstepping the truth.'

The House of Hillel say, 'One sings, "Beautiful and graceful bride!" whether this is true or not.'

Said the House of Shammai to the House of Hillel, 'Supposing she is lame, or blind—does one still sing "Beautiful and graceful bride!"? Surely the Torah has said, "Keep thee from falsehood" [Exodus, 23: 7]?'

Said the House of Hillel to the House of Shammai, 'And if a man has made a bad purchase in the market, should one tell him that it is bad, or comfort him by telling him that it may turn out well? Have not the Sages said, "A man's mind should never be detached from his fellow-creatures."?'

Ketuvot, 16b

168

Rights of Workers

Rav says: 'A worker may withdraw his labour at any time, even in the middle of a day's work.'

What is the Scriptural authority for this right? It is the verse: 'For unto me the children of Israel are slaves.' They are slaves to God, but not to men, for that would make them the slaves of slaves.

Bava Metsia, 10a

Note. The question of Trade Unions does not arise explicitly in the Talmud, but medieval and modern codes, on the basis of the above saying, and other similar ones, view Trade Unions favourably and give them the same status as other representative bodies.

HIRING WORKMEN

He who hires workmen and tells them to start work early or to go on working late has no right to compel them to do this unless the local custom is to start work early and work late. If the local custom is to provide workmen with food, he must do so. If the local custom is to provide them with a sweet course, he must do so.

It once happened that Rabbi Johanan ben Mattia said to his son, 'Go out and hire some workmen for us.' He went and hired some and undertook to give them food. He came back to his father and told him what he had agreed. Said Rabbi Johanan, 'My son, even if you made them a feast like Solomon in his time, you would not have discharged your obligation to

169

them, for they are the children of Abraham, Isaac and Jacob. But hurry before they start work and tell them that by "food" you mean bread and beans.'

Said Rabban Simeon ben Gamaliel, 'This was not necessary, for everything goes according to the local custom.'

Bava Metsia, 7: 1

Kindness to Animals

Rabbi Judah the Prince suffered for many years from stones in the kidneys, which caused him great pain. This suffering came to him through a certain incident. A calf was being taken to the slaughter. It broke away, hid under the long robe of Rabbi Judah the Prince, and wept.

Said Rabbi Judah the Prince to the calf, 'Go, for you were created for this.'

Upon this, it was said in Heaven, 'Since he does not show pity, suffering will come upon him.'

After thirteen years, his sufferings departed. This also happened through an incident. One day, his maidservant was sweeping the house and found some kittens. She was about to throw them out, but he stopped her, saying, 'Leave them, for it is written, "His tender mercies are over all his works" [Psalms, 145: 9].'

Upon this, it was said in Heaven, 'Since he is merciful, let mercy be shown to him.'

Bava Metsia, 85a

SOME LAWS ON KINDNESS TO ANIMALS

Prevention of suffering of animals is a biblical law, and therefore takes precedence of all rabbinical laws (e.g. rabbinical laws relating to the Sabbath may be broken in order to prevent an animal from suffering).

Shabbat, 128b

171

Rav Judah said in the name of Rav: 'A man is forbidden to eat before he gives food to his animals.'

Berakhot, 40a

The Seven Laws of the Sons of Noah are:
    to have laws of justice;
    to refrain from blasphemy;
    to refrain from idolatry;
    from murder; from robbery;
    from eating flesh cut from a living animal.
    Rabbi Hidka added: 'Also from castrating animals.'

Sanhedrin, 56a

Note. The Seven Laws of the Sons of Noah are the basis of an International Law, discussed and elaborated in the Talmud.

A person must not acquire a domestic animal or bird unless he has arranged for it to have suitable food.

Yerushalmi, Yevamot, 14d

THE LAND

The Mishnah begins with the Order of 'Seeds' because in it are the commandments relating to agriculture, upon which all life depends.

Moses Maimonides,
Commentary on the Mishnah

Rabban Johanan ben Zakki used to say, 'If you are holding a seedling in your hands ready to plant, and you hear a cry, "The Messiah has come!", first finish planting your seedling, and then go and meet the Messiah.'

He also used to say, 'If the young men say to you, "Let us go and build the Temple", do not listen to them. But if the old say to you, "Come, let us destroy the Temple," listen to them. For the building of youths is destruction, and the destruction of the old is building.'

Avot d'Rabbi Nathan B, Ch. 31

A CONVERSATION ON AGRICULTURE

MANKOWITZ   Let's discuss this saying of Rabbi Johanan ben Zakkai: 'If you are holding a seedling in your hand ready to plant, and you hear a cry, "The Messiah has come!", first finish planting your seedling, and then go and meet the Messiah.' Now that seems to me to indicate that it is more important to cultivate the fruitfulness of the land even than to greet the ultimate event of human history. What's your explanation of why this extraordinary importance is placed upon land cultivation in the Talmudic writings?

MACCOBY   Rabbi Johanan's saying is expressed in a paradoxical, exaggerated style which is typical of the Talmud—Christian readers have met this style in some of the sayings of Jesus recorded in the Gospels. I don't think that Rabbi Johanan is opposing the importance of agriculture to the importance of the Messiah. The point is this: why do Jews look forward to the coming of the Messiah? The meaning of the coming of the Messiah, as Rabbi Johanan indicates, lies in the planting of the seed. The Messiah is the culmination of the whole process which comprises the great adventure of agriculture. I would say that Judaism is, of all the religions of the world, the religion and philosophy of agriculture. This is very much against the idea that many people have of the Jews. There is the idea that the Jews are a commercial people, town-dwellers who make their living out of the surface of a culture rather than being peasants and working on the land. But this particular picture of the Jews is relatively recent in Jewish history, because of adverse circumstances. Even during the long period in Europe when the Jews were legally prevented from owning land, their Biblical and Talmudic studies were all centred round agriculture, and their ideal remained to dwell in peace, as the prophet says, 'each man under his vine and under his fig-tree'.

MANKOWITZ   What about the picture sometimes put forward by anti-Semites that the Jews are essentially a desert people, a bunch of nomads who captured the fertile land of Canaan and turned it into their land, but never really lost their desert approach to life?

MACCOBY   In a sense, this is true. The reason why the Jews love the land so much is that they have never forgotten the desert. To them, the land was not just something they took for granted; it was the Promised Land, the land they were hungry for, the land which was the end of the long travail of crossing the desert. So the Jews, in their rituals, constantly remind themselves of the desert—for example, in the Feast of Tabernacles, when they leave their houses and eat in a tem-

176

porary booth, to remind themselves of the travels in the wilderness.

MANKOWITZ Would you say that the Jews are in love with the land?

MACCOBY Yes, there *is* a sexual element in it. The land is the female element in Judaism. The land is not the mother—that would be a nomadic, dependent attitude—so much as the lover or bride, who expects not adoration or helpless dependency but proper cultivation, and *husbandry*.

MANKOWITZ But is there not a Hebrew expression, *am ha-aretz*, which means literally 'people of the land', but has come to mean an ignorant person or boor? This suggests that, even in the Jewish tradition, the peasant is despised.

MACCOBY In some parts of the Talmud, which was written after the loss of Jewish statehood, one can see the beginnings of a withdrawal from the land. But the Biblical attitude is never lost—as when Rabbi Eliezer says, 'Someone who does not own and cultivate land is not a man.' This is the contrary of other cultures, where the very definition of being an aristocrat, a noble person, is that you don't cultivate the land. In Judaism, if you don't cultivate land, you are cut off from fulfilling a large part of the Law; for example, the laws of the Corner and the Forgotten Sheaf and the Fallow Year and the forbidden mixtures. You are not able to come to grips with that part of the moral law which concerns human relationships with the land. I think that if we realize that Judaism is a religion which has agriculture as its central theme, this helps us to make sense of the concept of the Messiah and the Messianic Age. It is an age in which the great adventure of agriculture comes to its culmination and the earth really flowers. It is not a concept of exploiting the earth, or of exploiting one class of men, the peasant class, so that superior people can wait till the crop is full and then steal it—

that is the basis and philosophy of all aristocratic societies and religions. In Judaism, the people who do the work are the aristocrats.

MANKOWITZ How apposite this is, I think, to our world situation, where even formerly affluent parts are on the edge of becoming members of the Third World, the deprived section of the world; because of overpopulation, and because our technological policies have pushed us into a more and more exploitative attitude towards natural sources of wealth and strength. If the Talmudic attitude were applied, every group of people would have a physical relationship with the land, whatever else they did. Children, factory-workers, students —all would spend part of their time producing the food that they eat. Each community would be substantially self-supporting, and the overall productivity of the earth would be infinitely greater than it is. Instead of which, hardly anyone concerns himself with producing the food that we consume every day. Most of us are involved in service or leisure functions, or in factory-type activities. The Talmud postulates a totally different attitude towards the way in which men should live and derive their life from the earth. To me, this is the most relevant piece of advice and wisdom that we've struck in our discussion.

I'm reminded, by what you say about the traditional Jewish attitude that a man who doesn't relate to the land is not a man, of my grandfather. I spent a great deal of time with him as a child, and he greatly influenced my basic thinking about life. He was an immigrant in the East End of London. He'd come from Russia, where he had a small piece of land which he cultivated, and from which he sold the surplus produce. In England, he had a little shop, with a place where everybody lived above it. And out back was a tiny piece of dirt, made of soot and shards and rubbish from the midden that London had been for hundreds of years. And in that yard, he kept two goats, about thirty hens, two or three geese, a few ducks, and there were always animals there. He couldn't live without the feeling that he had a direct relationship with land and the basic sources of food and the animals who provided through him for his family. And throughout his life, he did this. So my feeling, as a child, was that out back of whatever activity we are thrust into, there is a small triangular piece of unpromising dirt which contains in itself the essence of our lives. And we must dig for this essence to be released. I'm glad to find the source of this feeling is indeed in the Talmud.

MACCOBY   I'd just like to add one word to that. One of the things that is unique in the Jewish tradition is that in it, the peasant who works the land is not stupid. The peasant can be very, very intelligent. This is the tradition which has been revived in the *kibbutzim*—the community of peasant-intellectuals, which we find depicted in the Babylonian and Palestinian Talmuds. And this is at least an approach to an answer to our present quandary —which is that we are being overwhelmed by a huge machine. Human intelligence can surely give us the benefit of technology in such a way that we are not destroyed by it. Nowadays technology has reached a point at which it is possible not to need the great machine, which we tend like frenzied slaves, as in Charlie Chaplin's film. It's possible for technology to provide highly advanced machines which will be helpful to agriculture in small units rather than in a great impersonal commune.

Leaving a Corner
for the Poor

THE CORNER OF THE FIELD

The Torah says (Leviticus, 19: 9): 'And when ye reap the harvest of your land, thou shalt not wholly reap the corner of thy field, neither shalt thou gather the gleaning of thy harvest. And thou shalt not glean thy vineyard, neither shalt thou gather the fallen fruit of thy vineyard; thou shalt leave them for the poor and for the stranger: I am the Lord your God.' The Mishnah, in the tractate called 'Peah', gives legal body to these precepts, showing how they were carried out in practice. For example, one must leave the 'corner' of each field to be harvested by the poor, but what exactly is the definition of a 'field'?

He who sows his field with one kind of seed, though he makes up of it two threshing-floors, need separate off only one 'corner' for the poor. If he sows his field with two kinds of corn, then even if he employs only one threshing-floor, he must separate off two 'corners'. If, however, the two kinds of corn are merely different kinds of wheat: one threshing-floor—one 'corner'; two threshing-floors—two 'corners'.

The following serve as dividing-lines for purposes of separating the 'corner': a stream, a pool, a private road, a public road, a public path, or a private path in constant use in summer and the rainy season, fallow land, newly-cultivated land, and a different seed. If one cut young corn for fodder, the reaped space serves as a dividing-line; so says Rabbi Meir. But the Sages say, 'Only if it is re-ploughed.'

Mishnah, Peah, 2: 5

Waiting for Rain

If the 17th of Marheshvan has arrived, and no rain has fallen, individuals of special merit begin to observe a three-day fast. They may eat and drink after nightfall, and they are allowed to work, wash themselves, anoint themselves, wear shoes and have intercourse.

If the 1st of Kislev has come, and rain has still not fallen, the Court decrees a three-day fast for the congregation. They may eat and drink after nightfall, and are allowed to work, wash themselves, anoint themselves, wear shoes and have intercourse.

If these days have passed, and their prayers have not been answered, the Court decrees a further three-day fast for the congregation. They may not eat after nightfall, and they are not allowed to work, wash themselves, anoint themselves, wear shoes, or have intercourse, and the bath-houses are closed.

If these days have passed, and their prayers have not been answered, the Court decrees a further seven-day fast, during which the Shofar (ram's horn) is blown and the shops are closed, in addition to the previous observances. The shops may be partially opened on Mondays after dark, and may be open all day on Thursdays in honour of the Sabbath.

If these days have passed, and their prayers have not been answered, they diminish business, building and planting, betrothals and weddings, and greetings to one another, as people who are under the displeasure of God. Individuals of special merit continue to fast until the end of Nisan. If rain falls after that, it is a sign of God's curse (for the wheat harvest will be spoilt).

Mishnah, Ta'anit, 1:4

Note. Three-day fast . . . seven-day fast: *these were not continuous fasts. Fasting took place only on Mondays and Thursdays.*

First-Fruits

How do they separate the First-fruits? A man goes down in the midst of his field and sees a fig that has ripened or a cluster of grapes that has ripened or a pomegranate that has ripened; he binds it round with reed-grass and says, 'Behold, these are First-fruits.'

How do they take up the First-fruits to Jerusalem? The Representatives of a group of towns would gather in the constituency-town, and spend the night in the market-place, not entering the houses; and in the early morning the Leader of the Representatives would call out, 'Arise and let us go up to Zion unto the Lord our God' [Jeremiah, 31: 6].

Those who were near to Jerusalem would bring fresh figs and dates, and those who were far would bring dried figs and raisins. And before them would go the ox for the peace-offering, with its horns overlaid with gold and a wreath of olive-leaves on its head. The flute would play before them until they reached the vicinity of Jerusalem. When they reached the vicinity of Jerusalem, they sent messengers before them and arranged their First-fruits into wreaths. The chief priests and the chief Levites and the treasurers of the Temple would come out to meet them, in numbers commensurate with the size of the incoming party; and all the craftsmen of Jerusalem would stand before them and greet them, 'Our brothers, the men of such-and-such a place, welcome.'

The flute continued to play before them until they reached the Temple Mount. When they reached the Temple Mount, even King Agrippa would take a basket on his shoulder and carry it as far as the Temple Courtyard.

Mishnah, Bikkurim, 3: 1

Note. Here the Mishnah recalls the role of the Temple in the celebration of agriculture. The nostalgia which is an important ingredient in the whole Talmud is evident; nothing must be forgotten of the way things were done before the destruction of the Temple and the Jewish State; if these things could no longer be done, then at least the story of how they were done could be preserved and studied, so that at the coming of the Messiah, they could be put into operation immediately.

The scene of the procession recalls Keats's 'Ode on a Grecian Urn':

To what green altar, O mysterious priest,
Lead'st thou that heifer lowing at the skies,
And all her silken flanks with garlands drest?
What little town by river or sea shore,
Or mountain-built with peaceful citadel,
Is emptied of this folk, this pious morn?

The idyllic scene includes an allusion to King Agrippa (Herod Agrippa, the playboy friend of Caligula and Claudius, who was instrumental in bringing Claudius to the imperial throne and was rewarded by being made King of Judaea). Herod Agrippa in his short reign (41–44 CE) became, surprisingly, an ideal king in the eyes of the Pharisees, who had clashed with his ruthless grandfather, Herod the Great.

183

The Temple

The compound forming the incense consisted of balm, onycha, galbanum and frankincense, in quantities weighing seventy manehs each; of myrrh, cassia, spikenard and saffron, each sixteen manehs by weight; of costus, twelve; of aromatic bark, three; and of cinnamon, nine manehs; of lye obtained from a species of leek, nine kavs; of Cyprus wine, three seahs and three kavs: though, if Cyprus wine was not available, old white wine might be used; of salt of Sodom, the fourth part of a kav; and of the herb which causes smoke [maaleh ashan], just a pinch. Rabbi Nathan says, 'Also a pinch of the herb kippath, that grows by the Jordan.'

Kerithoth, 6a

THE CHAMBERS

The chambers to the south were the Wood Chamber, the Wheel Chamber, and the Chamber of Hewn Stone.

The Wood Chamber—Rabbi Eliezer ben Jacob said: 'I forget what it was used for.' Abba Saul said, 'It was the chamber of the High Priest and it lay behind the other two; and the roof of the three of them was on the same level.'

The Wheel Chamber—the cistern was there, and a wheel was set over it, and from it they drew all the water-supply for the Temple Court.

The Chamber of Hewn Stone—there the Great Sanhedrin of Israel used to sit and judge the priests; and if a blemish was found in any priest, he used to clothe himself in black and veil

184

himself in black and depart. But if no blemish was found in him, he clothed himself in white and veiled himself in white, and went in and ministered with his brethren the priests. And they kept it as a festival-day since no blemish was found in the seed of Aaron. And thus they used to say, 'Blessed be God, blessed be He! that no blemish has been found in the seed of Aaron!'

Middot, 5: 4

Rights of the Public

Our Rabbis taught: Joshua made ten conditions when he handed over the Land to the children of Israel as an inheritance:

1. that cattle should be allowed to pasture in woods;
2. that people should be allowed to gather wood in private fields;
3. that people should be allowed to gather grasses for fodder from all fields except one in which fenugreek is growing;
4. that people should be allowed to cut off shoots in all places, except for the stumps of olive trees;
5. that if a spring emerges for the first time, it may be used by the townspeople;
6. that people should be allowed to fish with a rod or nets in the Sea of Tiberias, provided that they do not set up fishing-bays, which would interfere with shipping;
7. that people should be allowed to ease themselves at the back of a fence even in a field full of saffron;
8. that the public should be allowed to use the paths in private fields until the coming of the second rain;
9. that the public should be allowed to turn aside from the main road, if it has become hard and lumpy, and walk on the part of private fields adjacent to the road;
10. that anyone who has lost his way in the vineyards may cut his way through to find the road;
11. that if anyone falls dead, his corpse acquires possession of the land on which it lies and has a right to be buried there.

But these are eleven conditions, not ten! One of them (no. 8) was added by King Solomon.

But surely Joshua made some more conditions not mentioned above! Was there not the one mentioned by Rabbi Judah?—'When it is the season of removing animal dung, a man may

186

take his dung to a public place and heap it up there for thirty days, so that it may be trodden by the feet of men and animals, for it was on this condition that Joshua handed over the Land to the children of Israel as an inheritance.'

Moreover, was there not another condition mentioned by Rabbi Ishmael the son of Rabbi Johanan ben Beroka?—'If a swarm of bees has settled on a bough, the owner of the bees may enter his neighbour's field and cut off the bough together with the swarm, paying only the value of the bough, for it was on this condition that Joshua handed over the Land to the children of Israel as an inheritance.'

There is some difference of opinion about exactly how many conditions Joshua made. The opinion that he made ten conditions and no more is that of Rabbi Joshua ben Levi.

Bava Kamma, 80b

Note. Even though the Land was divided among the Tribes as an inheritance, property rights are limited. The rights of the public are regarded as anterior to the rights of private ownership; only on condition that the rights of the public were respected was the right to private property granted at all. This is in accordance with the Biblical attitude to private property as a gift of God, not an inherent human right. 'The land shall not be sold in perpetuity, for the land is Mine; for ye are strangers and settlers with Me' (*Leviticus, 25: 23*).

The Portion of the King

How did the king read his portion of the Law?

Once every seven years, on the first day of the Feast of Tabernacles, they used to build a wooden platform in the Temple Court, and on this the king sat.

The Beadle of the synagogue took a scroll of the law and handed it to the President of the synagogue, who handed it to the Vice-High-Priest, who handed it to the High Priest, who handed it to the king.

The king used to receive it standing, and read it out sitting, but King Agrippa received it standing and read it out standing, and the Sages praised him for this.

And when he reached the words, 'Thou shalt elect no foreigner as king' [Deuteronomy, 17: 15], his eyes flowed with tears (remembering his Edomite descent), but they called out to him, 'Do not fear, Agrippa, thou art our brother, thou art our brother, thou art our brother!'

Mishnah, Sotah, 7: 8

Note. The 'portion of the king' reads partly as follows (Deuteronomy, 17: 14–20): '... that his heart be not lifted up above his brethren, and that he turn not aside from the commandment, to the right hand or to the left, that he may prolong his days in his kingdom ...'

LIFE AND DEATH

Sanctity of Human Life

If an idolater should try to compel a Jew by force to transgress one of the commandments of the Torah on pain of death, he should transgress it rather than be killed, because the Torah says of the commandments, 'which if a man do, he will live by them'—by which it is implied that he should not die by them. And if he refuses to transgress and so dies, he is guilty of self-murder.

But this does not apply to the three great commandments which forbid idolatry, incest and murder. A man must be prepared to die rather than transgress these. And he must also be prepared to die even for lesser commandments than these, if the transgression of them is made into a public spectacle of the humiliation of Judaism. And if there is an official public campaign against Judaism, one must die for a lesser commandment even if one is required to violate it only in private.

If a man dies rather than violate a commandment, in a case where such death is required, he has 'sanctified the Name', like Daniel and Rabbi Akivah, and there is no higher degree to which a man can attain. But if he violates the commandment rather than die, he has 'profaned the Name'. Nevertheless, since he transgressed under compulsion, he is not liable to punishment, and it is hardly necessary to say that he is not subject to capital punishment, even if he killed somebody under compulsion. For there is no punishment, either corporal or capital, which applies except to one who transgresses by his own will, in full knowledge, and in the presence of witnesses.

Note. This summary by Maimonides is based on various passages

191

in the Talmud. These formulations have very often had tragic relevance and practical application in the course of Jewish history. They were often invoked, for example, during the Nazi holocaust. The following provision had special relevance at that time.

If idolaters said to Jews, 'Give us one of you to kill, or we will kill you all', they should all allow themselves to be killed, and not hand over a soul from Israel. But if they singled out one man by name, saying, 'Give us So-and-so to kill, or we will kill you all', they should hand him over, but only if he is actually guilty of a capital offence, like Sheba ben Bichri; but if not, they should all die rather than hand him over.

Maimonides, Mishneh Torah, Yesodei ha-Torah, 5: 1

CAPITAL CASES

The wording of the admonition given to witnesses in capital cases was as follows:

'Dismiss from your minds any idea that you may speak from guesswork or hearsay or second-hand or even on the authority of a trustworthy person. Know that we shall question you in a thorough, searching and probing manner. Know also that capital cases are different from non-capital cases; for whereas non-capital cases can be settled by money, in capital cases a witness may be responsible for the blood of the accused man and for the blood of his posterity until the end of time.

That is why God created one man, Adam, rather than creating the whole human race together. It was to show that if anyone causes a single soul to perish, it is as though he causes a whole world to perish; and if anyone saves alive a single soul, it is as if he had saved alive a whole world.'

Mishnah, Sanhedrin, 4: 5

ADAM AND THE HUMAN RACE

Other reasons have been given to explain why God created one man, Adam, rather than creating the whole human race together.

It was for the sake of peace among mankind, so that no one could say, 'My ancestor was greater than your ancestor.'

Again, it was to prevent heretics from saying, 'There are many gods, each of whom created some part of the human race.'

Again, it was to show the greatness of God, who could create the infinite variety of mankind from one man.

Again (Tosefta), it was that no sinner may say, 'I am a sinner by inheritance, being the descendant of sinners', and no saint may say, 'I am a saint by virtue of my descent from saints.'

Thus it is the duty of every man to declare, 'For my sake the world was created.'

Mishnah, Sanhedrin, 4: 5 and Tosefta, Sanhedrin, 8 3

Note. This passage, together with the previous one, contains the essence of Judaism. See Robert Gordis, 'A Basis for Morals', Judaism, Winter, 1976. 'The implications are clear: man's innate dignity is the source of his right to be different, which is the essence of freedom. The equality of men, as seen in their common origin, is the source of all men's right to justice.'

RED BLOOD

Once a man came to Rava and said to him, 'The governors of my town have ordered me to kill someone. If I do not kill him, the governors will kill me.'

Said Rava, 'Let them kill you, and do not kill another. How do you know that your blood is redder than his? Perhaps his blood is redder than yours.'

Sanhedrin, 74a

Right of Self-Defence

KILL HIM FIRST

The Torah has said, 'If someone comes to kill you, kill him first.'

Berakhot, 58a

TWO MEN IN THE DESERT

Two men are travelling in a desert, and in the hand of one of them is a bottle of water. If they both drink of the water, both of them will die; but if only one of them drinks, he will survive and reach civilization. What should the man with the water do?

Ben Petura said: 'It is better that they should both drink and they should both die; and one of them should not look on while his comrade dies. For Scripture says, "Thy brother shall live with thee" [Leviticus, 25: 36; i.e. if thy brother cannot live with thee, thou shouldst die with him].'

This was accepted until Rabbi Akiva came and taught: 'Your life comes before his life, for Scripture says, "Thy brother shall live with thee" [i.e. not at the expense of thy life].'

Bava Metsia, 62

194

Responsibility

NO AGENT FOR WRONG-DOING

If someone causes a fire through the agency of a person who cannot be held legally responsible (a deaf-mute, an imbecile, or a minor), he is responsible for the damage by the law of Heaven, but not by the law of man.

If someone causes a fire through the agency of a person who is legally capable, then the agent is responsible for the damage.

Why? Is there not a principle that the agent of a man is as himself?

Yes, but this principle does not hold in such a case, for there is another principle, 'There can be no agent for wrong-doing.' This principle is based on the reasoning, 'When the words of the Master [God] conflict with the words of the pupil, whose words should be obeyed?'

Kiddushin, 42b

Note. This is the Talmud's answer to those who excuse themselves for wrong-doing by saying, 'I was only obeying orders'. No human authority can outweigh basic moral imperatives, and a human being, provided he is in full possession of his faculties, is always responsible for his own actions.

AGENT OF MURDER

If someone says to his agent, 'Go and kill a certain person', the agent is liable to execution for the murder, not the sender.*

*This does not mean that the sender is free of punishment—only that he is not liable for capital punishment.

Shammai the Elder said on the authority of Haggai the prophet, 'His sender is liable, as in the case of King David and Uriah the Hittite.'

Said Rava, 'Even Shammai the Elder agrees that an agent is liable wherever he derives some benefit or pleasure from the crime—otherwise, a man who told someone to commit incest would be held responsible rather than the person who actually committed the incest.'

Kiddushin, 43a

196

SOME
CURIOSITIES

Rabbi Gamaliel's Telescope

Rabban Gamaliel had a tube through which he could see at a distance of two thousand cubits across land or sea.

Eruvin, 43b

The Child in the Womb

Rabbi Simlai discoursed as follows:

'What does an embryo resemble when it is in the womb? Folded writing-tablets. Its hands are against its temples, and its elbows are on its legs, and its heels are against its buttocks, and its head is between its knees. Its mouth is closed, and its navel is open, and it eats and drinks what its mother eats and drinks. It produces no excrement, for if it did, it would kill its mother.

When it comes out into the air of the world, what was closed becomes open, and what was open becomes closed—otherwise it would not be able to live a single hour.

When the child is in the womb, a light shines above its head, by which it can see from one end of the world to the other. Do not be amazed at this, for in dreams a man in Babylonia may see as far as Spain.

There are no days so steeped in happiness as the days spent in the womb.

While in the womb, the child learns the entire Torah, and knows it. But when the child enters the air of the world, an angel comes and strikes it on the mouth, and thus causes it to forget all the Torah it has learnt.

Niddah, 30b

The Barbarous Britons

'I will provoke them with a vile nation' [Deuteronomy, 32: 24]. It was taught: This refers to the barbarians of Britain who go about naked in public, for nothing is more objectionable to God than this.

Yevamot, 63b

Note. There is another reading according to which this saying refers to the savages of North Africa, not of Britain. If, however, the above reading is correct, it marks the rather inauspicious beginning of British-Jewish relations.

A CONVERSATION ON BARBAROUS BRITONS

MANKOWITZ   Let's take this passage about the barbarians of Britain who go about naked in public, which is something very objectionable to God. Why do you conclude that it is the barbarians of Britain specifically?

MACCOBY   I included that because I thought it would interest British readers to find that they had been mentioned in the Talmud, if not in very complimentary terms. Unfortunately, the reading is not quite certain—it is possible that the correct reading is not 'Britannia' but 'Mauretania'. There are many variant readings in the Talmud, especially in passages, such as this one, which appear more than once.

MANKOWITZ   What is 'Britannia' in Hebrew?

MACCOBY   Just a straightforward transliteration—'Britannia'. The existence of that remote island was, of course, well known to the rabbis of the Talmud.

MANKOWITZ   It's certainly true that the Celts who inhabited Britain went into battle stark naked. When they were not in battle they wore clothes of one sort or another, but they did take off their clothes to fight.

MACCOBY   I wonder if there was some mystical reason for this. Did they feel that they were under the special protection of their god if they went into battle naked?

MANKOWITZ   I think partly it was for sheer mobility, but also— as far as my superficial researches go—for toughness. They trained in the nude for battle and lived in groups together. Those who couldn't sustain the climate and the other trials died off, and those who were left must have been incredibly strong people. The Scots and the Irish today are so physically strong—it constantly amazes me, how strong the Irish are, despite hundreds of years of systematic deterioration.

I think that is why they deliberately went into battle nude.

MACCOBY   To develop hardiness, and also to prove their hardiness, they fought without armour?

MANKOWITZ   I think so. Another point is that they used to grease their bodies, so that they were very hard to hold on to.

MACCOBY   Didn't they use blue paint?

MANKOWITZ   Dr Raftery of the Dublin National Museum maintains that body painting was not practised by the Celts. He thinks it's a misreading of certain early documents which has attributed tattooing to them. There is an object, a wooden head—I talked to him about this recently—which shows face-markings very similar to the Maori face-markings, and a great deal of mistaken theory has been built on this one object. Raftery insists that the Celts did not tattoo and did not have body painting.

MACCOBY I see you have a great admiration for the naked Celts, whom the Talmud seems to have regarded as abominable. I wonder if we can venture a generalization. There were two kinds of culture in ancient times: the survival-of-the-fittest type of culture and the molly-coddling type of culture, of which, in a sense, the Jews were the chief example, since they set their faces against every type of weeding out of weaklings, holding, indeed, that weaklings must have the special protection of society. The Greeks and Romans used to expose infants who were weak or ailing, or even just because they were girls. The father was given absolute rights over the lives of his children. In Judaism, the exposure of infants was regarded as plain murder, and a father had no more rights over his children's lives than over any other people's lives. Now which is the best policy for survival, the survival-of-the-fittest policy, by which you weed out your weaklings, or the Jewish policy of never weeding out anybody? ˉ

MANKOWITZ Perhaps the Jewish assumption was that the weeding-out would be done by destiny—by the pogroms. After all those centuries—say three thousand years—the Jews number only about fourteen million. There's been some very efficient weeding there, despite the fact that the Jews have not gone in for exposing surplus babies and knocking off the old.

MACCOBY There's another point arising out of what you have said about the Celts and their nudity. The Jews have a great regard for the importance of the body, regarding it as the basis of the good life, yet as opposed to the Greeks and the Celts, they have always been very shy about exposing their bodies. This shyness has always been a feature of the Jewish culture. Of course, you might say it's a feature of Oriental culture generally. Arabs, too, regard it as a disgrace to be seen naked, whereas the Greeks had their Olympic Games in which the participants had to be naked. They gloried in the naked body and in portraying the gods as naked figures. This shocked the Jews, who were more shocked by the naturalistic Greek statues than by the stylized statues of other polytheistic nations.

MANKOWITZ   The Greeks made the body into a fantastic object, a wonderful object of art. But in the process, the experiences and sensations of the body became pretty thoroughly depersonalized. Caligula was a great admirer of Hellenistic works of art, but the value he placed upon the human body was so small that he could have one cut to pieces while he had his breakfast so he could be amused by the noises that the subject made. There is an actual non-valuation of the human being within the body, because the body itself has been raised to the level of idolatry. Because surely too great worship, too great pleasure in the beauty of a beautiful human body starts to become a form of idolatry. The psychological objection to idolatry is that idols are separated elements of human narcissism, and the narcissistic human individual is a deteriorating psychology, frequently a psychopathology.

MACCOBY   The Jews lived inside their bodies. They didn't put them outside as something to worship.

MANKOWITZ   I think the Jews respect the power of the body. It contains such power that you can't make an easy thing of it. You can't make a plaything of it, and you can't separate yourself from it in order to admire it. When you separate—when you violate the unity of the personality—you get idolatry of the parts.

204